FOREIGN LANGUAGE

How to use modern technology to effectively learn foreign languages

Special edition for students
of Japanese language

FOREIGN LANGUAGE. How to use modern technology to effectively learn foreign languages. Special edition for students of Japanese language

by Andrey Taranov

This book is a compilation of information about modern resources available to foreign language students. The purpose of this book is to help the reader to correctly select instructional materials and organize independent study of a foreign language. This edition contains recommendations for the use of both traditional methods as well as the latest multimedia technologies. The book gives great attention to vocabulary development – how to correctly study, review, and systematize foreign words.

Translated by Samuel James Pinson
www.pinsonlingo.com

ISBN 978-1-78314-812-7

T&P Books Publishing
www.tpbooks.com

FOREWORD

There is not, and never has been, a unified system that people could use to learn foreign languages. Each age of the world contributes its own changes to the learning process, introducing new ideas and technologies. We now live at a time when the quantity of language study resources and materials of every imaginable kind has reached a level that makes it difficult for somebody to determine which learning aids would be most suitable.

This book is a compilation of useful information about modern resources available to foreign language students. We will examine what makes a particular resource interesting and explore the strengths and weaknesses of each of them. In the book you will also find helpful advice on how to receive the greatest effect from the primary and supplemental materials that can be used in the learning process.

This book will help you determine the main goals and exercises associated with mastering a foreign language. These goals are always there. They simply need to be stated, analyzed, and ordered. In general, systemization and order are two of the main factors in mastering anything new, including foreign languages. When you understand what you want to achieve you will find it much easier to choose a path that will lead to success.

To those who doubt their abilities and believe themselves linguistically incapable, we confidently affirm that anybody can learn a foreign language. Incapable people don't exist. There are only different degrees of need for a language and different levels of opportunity for instruction. There are also a large number of learning aids and, often, a poor understanding of how to use them effectively. In this book, we will help you with this last point.

The importance of the study materials you expect to use is difficult to overstate. These are the raw inputs for producing a quality product – your knowledge. Don't think that everything comes easily to people who can speak multiple languages. Before beginning to study a new language, every polyglot will carefully gather good practical materials and review the resources that may be needed. Sometimes this takes months. And only afterward does he proceed to quickly and systematically learn the language.

Another thing about polyglots. They are lucky. They are internally motivated to compete with themselves. They try to outdo their own brain, to push its limits and reveal all of its capabilities. These "intellectual athletes" find new and still newer methods for obtaining improved results. This includes the use of modern technologies.

Even if everyone isn't able to become a polyglot, each person can learn one or two foreign languages well enough to converse and read books. Serious motivation is great – but when the wrong materials put you at a loss on every page, even the most enduring enthusiasm will be snuffed out. Your motivation must be constantly nurtured by the feeling that you are moving forward, that everything is working out. If that isn't happening, then the problem is probably not you, but rather the learning aids you are using.

First of all, try to calculate how much time you will spend studying a foreign language at home in a regular, calm environment, and what other minutes of free time you may have in the course of a day. Time on public transportation, breaks at work, even waiting in line – these can all be used effectively for a "linguistic workout". Each person will get her own study schedule based on her current lifestyle.

Once you understand where and under what circumstances you can study you can think about selecting learning materials. For stationary work at home, a certain set of materials will be appropriate. For language study on the road, it is better to choose a different collection of resources more suitable for "mobile learning". In this book we will examine some options for these sets of study materials.

When it comes to planning your studies, the beginning stage is always the same – to master the fundamentals, to acquire the most basic knowledge about the language. You can subsequently emphasize various aspects of the language, such as reading, conversational speech, aural comprehension, and writing. But the first step is similar for every language. On the pages of this book you will find helpful advice on how to correctly select materials for each stage of the learning process.

In addition to speaking about motivation and the importance of foreign languages, it should be stated that studying a language is work – but it is work aimed at self-development. This process is similar to bodybuilding, where you exercise persistently and see your results improve gradually. If great athletes impress others with their well-proportioned bodies, you too will amaze your friends and coworkers with your knowledge of a foreign language.

In general, knowledge of a foreign language gives several additional reference points for evaluating a person and his character. A person's knowledge of a foreign language implies that she has invested time in study, is diligent, goal-oriented, and knows how to accomplish the tasks at hand. Though they don't say it, employers prize this. They can see in that line on your resume an entire paragraph of favorable information. Knowing a language also gives you added credibility in the eyes of your coworkers and friends.

Another positive aspect of foreign language study is its effect on a person's mental capabilities in old age. According to research, people who diligently engage in mental effort are able to maintain clarity of mind and reason sensibly much longer in their advanced years. This includes teachers, for example, and it is fully applicable to people who are actively studying foreign languages.

We're confident that this book will help you develop your own effective learning system and give you another boost in this useful and fascinating exercise – learning a foreign language.

TABLE OF CONTENTS

METHODS AND TECHNIQUES 91

JAPANESE VOCABULARY 105

CONCLUSION 167

PRINTED MATERIALS

Part 1

Despite the rapid development of digital technology, traditional printed books remain an important part of learning a foreign language. This chapter explains the printed materials that are appropriate for use at various levels of learning. You'll also find a description of several types of dictionaries as well as information about electronic books.

1.1 BOOKS IN THE ORIGINAL

Alongside being able to speak and understand foreign speech, reading books in the original is a goal pursued by anybody studying a foreign language. In order to use unadapted books, especially at the beginning and intermediate levels, you must learn how to correctly select study materials.

Reading any original texts is good in that the reader can become fully immersed in the new linguistic environment, understand the peculiarities and features of the residents of another country, and become more familiar with their culture. It is in these books that you will find interesting turns of speech and set expressions that are actually used in real life.

The decision to include a book in your study plan should be based on a few basic points:

- your skill level in the language
- the work's literary genre
- the size of the book
- the book's type (printed or electronic)

If you have only just begun learning a language, you should refrain from trying to read any serious foreign works. No matter how interesting the book may be, it will be too hard to understand. Most difficult to read are historical novels, especially those with a maritime theme, and romantic dramas, which have a rich vocabulary to describe the myriad nuances of a character's state of mind.

You should master "original" reading using children's books intended for children from 6 to 12 years old. The words used in them will be very simple, but this is precisely what makes them powerful at the beginning stage.

Once you have acquired a vocabulary of 2,000-3,000 words, you can try to start reading small detective novels or short stories. Detective novels are great for learning a language. They usually aren't very long, and they have interesting plots and intriguing endings.

A 2,000-word vocabulary will only be enough to occasionally encounter a familiar word in the text. Let your goal be just that. At the beginning stages, the tasks you create for yourself shouldn't be any more complicated. If you try to translate the entire text, you will soon realize how exhausting that is. The most likely outcome is that you won't have the patience to make it all the way through to the end of the book.

To briefly summarize, we do not recommend beginning to read books in the original until your linguistic arsenal includes knowledge of the basic rules of grammar and a 4,000-5,000-word vocabulary. You can try reading children's books, but it would be better to emphasize reading special fiction books that have been adapted to your level.

The primary educational benefit of reading any text, including unadapted books, consists of augmenting your vocabulary, and identifying and repeating already familiar words. Reading also passively strengthens your knowledge of the rules of grammar, e.g. verb forms, superlatives, etc.

If you want to squeeze the most out of a text, try to memorize some passage from the book by heart. This is a great exercise for training your memory and developing your ability to speak. Doing so will help you reinforce several skills. But if you want to learn how to construct sentences really well, you are better off using a special technique, with progressively more complicated phrases and a consideration of the elements of grammar.

At an advanced stage, with a vocabulary of more than 9,000 words, you will be able to read any book for light reading. At that point you will understand the general meaning of every phrase. By then you will also have developed the ability to pick out the key words that are essential for putting together your "word puzzle".

At the intermediate stage of learning, the picture is somewhat different. Your vocabulary is actively augmented during this phase, so you will need to look up translations for a large number of unfamiliar words. This is interesting but labor-intensive. You will need an orderly system to ensure that your efforts to memorize new words are successful.

Creating such a system isn't difficult at all. You write out all new words and phrases in a notebook for new words (if you're working on paper) or enter them into a file created in any program that can work with tables. The paper version of a notebook for new words might be a writing pad, preferably spiral bound.

To keep your records properly, please note the following points: The words should be arranged in three columns: source words (words in your native language), the translation, and the transcription. If necessary, you can write notes to yourself in the third column instead of the transcription. Skip a line between every five words. The result will be a column split into small text blocks.

Arranging the words in this manner is intended to make reviewing them later more convenient. If you've mastered the rules of reading and are confident that your pronunciation is correct, then you can omit the transcription column. You may also want to include page numbers or chapter titles to more easily find words, if needed.

If you notice words having the same root while looking for a translation in a dictionary, you should write them down as well. Concepts related to each other by a single root are much more easily remembered. This means you will be able to expand your vocabulary significantly faster.

We previously stated that one of the main objectives of reading books in the original is to augment your vocabulary. If you assume this assertion is true, then the process of reading itself is just one phase of this work. The complete cycle of "academic reading of books in the original" consists of the following elements:

- initial reading (includes copying new words)
- learning new words (a separate set of actions)
- review of new words (using the notebook for new words)
- re-reading (self-testing and vocabulary review)

If desired, you can read aloud the new words and create a small audio dictionary out of them. This will be very useful if you grow tired of working with printed materials or are on the road.

Repetition and reading intensity greatly affect how well new words are memorized. The rule is simple: review as often as possible; read as much as possible. Then reading books in the original will become a reality for you much sooner.

Summary: Reading books in the original requires significant linguistic experience – knowledge of the basic rules of grammar and a vocabulary of 4,000-5,000 words. Therefore, at the beginning stage this should be limited to working with special adapted literature.

1.2 ADAPTED BOOKS

Adapted books are literary works that have been specially developed for learning a foreign language. These books are usually recommended for reading at the beginning and intermediate levels of learning. In this section we will examine the particulars of this educational resource.

When selecting an adapted study aid, pay attention to the author's nationality. It is better if the book is adapted by a native speaker of the language. This will increase your confidence in the publication and consequently improve the overall results.

Adapted books have a number of positive qualities, because they are created by people who understand well your goals and challenges. Some publishers offer books with several adaptations designed for different levels of skill in a language.

The glossary of difficult words typically provided at the end of adapted books can be considered a huge plus, as can the various explanatory notes on geographical names, historical events, or set expressions.

Bear in mind that the books most frequently offered for sale are based on works by well-known classical authors. For example, for the English language this includes books by Arthur Conan Doyle, Agatha Christie, and Mark Twain. You will encounter a large number of obsolete and rare words in the original versions of these books. The adaptation gives you a simplified alternative that only contains useful, frequently-encountered words and phrases.

Thanks to the fact that adapted works are always quite short, you will easily read all the way through to the end. After reading you will have a modest number of new words that will be remembered without difficultly because you will clearly understand the context in which you encountered them.

You may also see adapted books for sale accompanied by an audio recording of the text. This is an excellent addition that makes it possible to review new words more often and helps improve comprehension of foreign speech. If your book is in electronic form you can try listening to it using text-to-speech (speech synthesis) technology.

Summary: Adapted books are a great educational resource for the beginning and intermediate levels. They are often furnished with supplementary information and a built-in dictionary of difficult words.

1.3 CLASSIC PRINTED DICTIONARIES

In this section we will examine the use of classic printed dictionaries to find the meaning of foreign words. The publications are typically large and expensive. Today they are gradually being supplanted by electronic dictionaries and translators. Nevertheless, they remain in demand, especially for rare languages.

A big advantage of large printed dictionaries lies in the fact that they are high-quality, trustworthy publications which have been carefully reviewed. Many large dictionaries began to be created in the 70s-80s and even earlier. They are periodically updated with modern words and checked for inaccuracies.

Using printed dictionaries

At any level of learning, you should have a large dictionary (printed or electronic) with as many words as possible. A good dictionary for translating books in the original should contain at least 100,000 words. Dictionaries with fewer words can be used at the beginning stages to translate uncomplicated texts. But you will soon constantly come up against words that you cannot translate, and in the end you will have to acquire a more serious reference book.

Large dictionaries sometimes contain more than a thousand pages. To speed up finding words we recommend making tabs with the letters of the alphabet and sticking them to the first page for each letter. Doing so will significantly accelerate the process of finding the part of the dictionary you are looking for.

Bear in mind that due to their large size, you will only use these dictionaries when you are stationary: at home or at work. So if you are frequently on the move and plan to study a language while traveling, you should consider also buying a good electronic dictionary.

People sometimes use small dictionaries to actively add to their vocabulary, that is, they study words directly from the dictionary. This can be done, but these publications are very inconvenient for review and self-testing. The layout of classical dictionaries assumes they will be used as reference books.

Small dictionaries (up to 50,000 words) rarely perform the role of a full-fledge dictionary, but they may have another application. You can use them to create your own personal word list for study.

You can find your own important and interesting new words in the dictionary and add them to your notebook. For example, if there are a thousand words in the dictionary that begin with the letter "A", then copy down one hundred common words and learn them. This isn't the most effective method, but it may work for you. You need to keep a separate notebook for new words from this sort of dictionary. Leave a few empty pages for each letter in case you want to add something later.

Summary: Large printed dictionaries are gradually being displaced by new technologies, but they will remain a source of high-quality, trustworthy information for a long time to come. From the very beginning, it is best to have as big a dictionary as possible, with at least 100,000 words.

1.4 TOPICAL DICTIONARIES

Topical dictionaries of generally used words are a separate category of publications which is one of the best ways to augment your vocabulary and memorize foreign words. The concept behind these dictionaries is to divide all the words in the publication into different topics. For example, under the topic "family" you would find the words "mother", "brother", "relative", etc. The topic "city" would include "bank", "fountain", "post office", and so on.

Topical dictionaries may be distinguished by parameters such as the number of words. A book containing 2,000-3,000 words will suffice for the beginning level. A dictionary with 10,000 entries is enough for the intermediate level. You may occasionally encounter impressive topical dictionaries for sale with 25,000-40,000 words. This books are useful, but they include a large number of rare concepts that you probably won't need at the beginning and intermediate levels.

Unlike ordinary classic dictionaries, which are used to look up the meaning of unfamiliar words, topical dictionaries have great potential for use as a study aid. Not only can they be used to find out about new words, they also actively facilitate memorizing them.

A fundamental part of an effective language learning system is to work with new words correctly – selecting them, ordering them, learning them, and reviewing them. At the beginning stage topical dictionaries may become your primary source of such words, which have been carefully organized and gathered into one place.

In this book you will often encounter the idea that all new words and expressions should be put into a single database. It would be best for you to create this database as an electronic spreadsheet in Excel or any other program that supports working with lists.

You can find new words from a wide variety of sources – books, movie subtitles, textbooks, online articles, etc. Your objective is to ensure that new words are not lost and that you always have access to them for regular review.

Using topical dictionaries for study

You can use a topical dictionary as a ready-made notebook for new words. In other words, you can memorize and review words directly in the dictionary. This is especially useful to quickly build up your vocabulary at the beginning stage.

But no matter how good your printed dictionary is, we still advise transferring all new words from a topical dictionary to your general database of words on a computer. This will give you a slew of new abilities: search and sort words, print desired parts of your list, remove duplicates, etc.

There is no need to create a strict algorithm for using topical dictionaries to learn words, but a rough outline might look like this:

- select a topic in the dictionary (you can follow the order in which they are presented, but this is not required)
- copy all or part of the words from this topic into your electronic database
- perform a set of actions to memorize these words (using a printed dictionary and computer printouts or the screen)
- periodically review all recently learned words

A topical dictionary will help in this work, but how well the words are memorized will be affected by several other factors such as the level of development of your abilities to master new information and the amount of time spent actively studying.

Summary: Topical dictionaries can be an important source for quickly building up your vocabulary at the beginning stage. They are useful for both memorizing new words and reviewing them.

1.5 VISUAL DICTIONARIES

A visual dictionary is a type of topical dictionary that contains words, translations, and images (photographs or drawings) that illustrate each concept. These books make it possible to create more enduring associations thanks to the involvement of visual memory. There are two main types of visual dictionaries, which are primarily distinguished by the placement of the images and the text.

In the first the name and translation of an object are given next to the image. That is, each page contains a certain number of pictures with captions. Sometimes a page will depict a complicated subject – for example, an automobile – with arrows indicating the separate parts: roof, wheels, headlights, etc.

This sort of visual dictionary is a reference book. It may have a good layout and contain beautiful, high-quality illustrations, but additional steps must be taken for it to fully perform its function. The arrangement of such a visual dictionary doesn't facilitate effective review, because all the information – the source word, the translation, and the image – are right before your eyes.

In order to get the most out of this type of book, you must copy all the desired words into your database for subsequent study, e.g. use the book as another source of words to augment your vocabulary. You will study and review the words in your notebook for new words, but the dictionary will help you create and reinforce a visual representation of each word.

In the second type of visual dictionary the images and text are arranged on different pages. This is usually on the same spread, with numbered images on the left side and image descriptions on the right. These dictionaries frequently contain black-and-white images rather than color images, but this doesn't make them any less functional.

In terms of actively augmenting your vocabulary, these publications provide huge opportunities. You get a great topical dictionary with pictures, which make it highly convenient to memorize and review new words.

You can use such a book at any time to practice recalling the meaning of words based on the images. To do this, you should cover the page or the part of the page with the words. You can always check yourself against the correct answer for difficult words.

Bear in mind that visual dictionaries usually contain concepts expressed by common nouns, i.e. words that have an easily identifiable visual representation.

These dictionaries will have few verbs, adjectives, and words signifying abstract concepts.

Despite the fact that the book's contents will be conveniently organized, we still advise transferring all interesting words to your notebook for new words. This can take a lot of work, but it is necessary in order to store your vocabulary in one place.

Summary: Visual dictionary are great sources for adding to your vocabulary. A big advantage of such books is that they enhance the memorization of new words and strengthen a "concept-object" association thanks to the visual examples.

1.6 VOCABULARY FLASH CARDS

Learning foreign words using flash cards is one of the oldest ways to build and enrich vocabulary. In the past these cards only existed in printed form. Today you can find a multitude of flash-card apps for mobile phones and memo-card-like computer programs.

The standard technique for using printed flash cards, in which the source word is written on one side and the translation on the other, can be considered obsolete and inadequate for modern learning. Flash cards can be used by people who are firmly accustomed to printed educational materials and willing to carry around a big deck of them.

One disadvantage of traditional flash cards is that you are forced to learn the words provided by the publisher. However, this isn't always the best selection of words, not to mention the fact that it in no way accounts for your personal skill level.

The cards are practically always picked based on measures of frequency and contain the most commonly used words. This may be appropriate for the most basic level, because at the first stage of learning there is a need for a fundamental source to build your vocabulary.

We suggest using the flash-card technique somewhat differently. Flash cards will become more beneficial if you make them yourself. And only for words that require effort to remember. With time you will accumulate a small selection of difficult words that you can review.

A variant of this technique is to write hard-to-remember words on sticky pieces of paper. By attaching a paper with a word where you will be sure to see it several times a day – on the mirror, for example – you will have sufficient opportunity to repeat the word.

In order to construct a proper system for working with words, we once again recommend that you create a single "reservoir" for all of the new words you encounter in your learning – your own personal word database. Without this system, some of your words will be on flash cards, some in a textbook, and some elsewhere still.

If you have a large number of unorganized words, you will have difficulty reviewing them, and that is one of the most important factors in reinforcing long-term memory. You will also find it difficult to determine the total number of words that you already know. Understanding how far you've come is necessary to reap an added boost of motivation in studying a language.

Thus, if you use ready-made flash cards, we recommend copying them all into your notebook for new words. You can make a special section in it called "Flash Cards". Then you will know precisely how much your vocabulary has grown. Incidentally, the very process of copying the words also promotes memorization.

Now you can review the words using both the flash cards as well as your note-book, if convenient. Additionally, you can make your own audio recording of the words on the flash cards to make the review process even more effective.

Summary: Vocabulary flash cards are a classic method for building your vocabulary. In today's world, we suggest using them only when working with difficult words that require effort to remember.

1.7 TEXTBOOKS AND AIDS

A multitude of different resources and educational materials are typically employed when learning a foreign language. Each of them has its own objective, and each of them supports development of specific skills. For example, the radio provides the opportunity to improve listening comprehension. Adapted books help in learning to read and review new words. Watching foreign films with subtitles reinforces your linguistic experience in a holistic fashion.

With time, each person forms his or her own set of study resources. Some of them will be basic, and some will be supplementary. The higher the quality of this collection, the better the result you will obtain.

Textbooks are a mandatory part of any foreign language course. In this section we will talk about what types of textbooks exist and how to choose an aid that is appropriate specifically for you.

Unfortunately, among all of varied learning materials available for sale it is difficult to identify one that would meet every requirement. For example, some textbooks expound verbs well, while others provide a good explanation of phonetics. Still others will have lots of useful exercises, but they can only be completed with an instructor.

Textbooks can differ from one another in many respects. Authors place different weight on the various elements of a language and apply different methods and principles in conveying the material. Finally, each textbook has its own layout, which can also either help or hinder learning.

Every textbook should include theory and exercises. The theory part is a description of the rules of grammar, tables of word endings, and instructions on the use of various words and expressions. The exercises serve to encourage retention of what is presented in theoretical sections.

Books that only contain theory are frequently referred to as textbooks. However, these aids cannot be considered full-fledged textbooks; more accurately, they are reference books. These too can be helpful, but using them means you have to independently process the information received. This can be done, but it will require effort and certain linguistic skills.

It is often difficult to determine how good a textbook is when you buy it. Only after carefully studying it at home and working through several exercises is possible to know if you like it or no. Most likely, you will decide to acquire 3-4 different textbooks and use each of them on occasion.

If you plan to study on your own, then the textbook shouldn't leave you unclear about anything. Good exercises are constructed in such a way that you can always check your answers. After each textbook exercise it is essential that you have a clear understanding of the material presented.

We will mention several of the most common standard exercises:

- multiple choice questions
- multiple choice cloze test
- open cloze test
- matching

All of these exercises help promote mastery of the material being studied and introduce variety into the learning process. But it is best to have a large number of examples for each rule and their translation into your native language. Being able to freely translate these phrases is a sign that you have truly mastered the material.

Different types of textbooks

Textbooks should preferably be written in your native language. There are a number of aids where all of the content, including supplementary text, explanatory notes, and exercise instructions are given in the foreign language. Several authors feel that such an approach is an additional aspect of "deep immersion in the linguistic environment." The may be appropriate for people working with an instructor, but for independent students, it only complicates the learning process.

You may encounter study aids with titles like "Spanish in 3 Months" or "Learn to Speak French in a Week." These books, whose titles typically do not reflect actual results, are unique in their content. A "Spanish in 3 Months" book does indeed assume that studying it will take three months. But whether or not you will have learned the language in that time is an entirely different question.

A "Learn to Speak ... in a Week" book will only teach you how to pronounce the material presented in the book. You will probably not learn how to independently construct phrases and create meaningful sentences (i.e. what is usually implied by being able to "speak") from a book like that. You can consider such a publication to be a "study phrasebook" that will to some degree help you fine-tune your pronunciation, assuming the book includes a good audio recording.

In general, these study aids are more suitable for repetitive use by people who are already fairly proficient at studying foreign languages. Or people with some sort of extraordinary memory. However, for most people they will simply be a minor supplementary reference.

There may be benefit in publications with a detailed development of a specific grammar topic or an in-depth look at using a particular part of speech. For example, Spanish verbs or imperatives. These aids are usually small booklets that expound the subject in detail, whereas it will be presented in condensed form in a large textbook.

In general, a classic textbook assumes the book will be divided into a certain number of lessons, each of which contains a short text, new words, a description of several elements of grammar, and exercises to reinforce them. The content of the entire book is organized from easiest to hardest, in terms of the vocabulary and the peculiarities of the specific language.

These textbooks were initially created for an instructor working with students, and were designed for a rather long learning period, typically one year – sometimes even longer. During the course of the lessons, the teacher supplements the textbook with a large body of other materials, i.e. newspaper articles, video clips, audio recordings.

Using these publications, the learning process moves forward slowly, with a little time spent each day on exercises. You gradually learn new grammar rules and slowly build your vocabulary. If you use such a textbook to study independently, you will most likely encounter a large number of confusing points or vague statements. This is due to the fact that the book's approach assumes the assistance of an instructor who can answer any question.

In our view, the ideal textbook consists of a package that includes a printed book, an electronic version, and a large number of audio- and video materials. The textbook should assume zero knowledge of the language and be designed for active, independent study over the course of six months. The study materials should also include intermediate and final exams for self-testing.

Summary: Textbooks are important in the process of learning a foreign language. They give foundational information on grammar rules, spelling, and phonetics. There is no such thing as a perfect textbook. They all have their weaknesses and strengths.

1.8. LIST OF THE LANGUAGE'S GRAMMAR TOPICS

Each language has a certain number of grammar rules and topics that are necessary to fully master it. There aren't so many as it may seem at first glance. We recommend that you take the time to create a complete list of as many of these elements as you can find for the language you are studying. This list will show you the overall volume of information that must be learned, and it will form the basis for building a clear system for studying grammar.

The list should be created on a computer. First, enter every topic, one after another, from every possible source. You can probably find many such lists on the Internet. The next step is to sort this information into a specific order, preferably by part of speech. In other words, you would put everything related to verbs into a "Verbs" section, and so on. Your search will yield a list of 100-200 items. Some of them may be redundant – you can delete these. The rest of the list is what you need to learn. It's a lot of information which should be assimilated gradually, so don't be frightened.

Your list of grammar topics will be helpful in accomplishing a great number of tasks. First of all, you can use it as a tool to gauge your progress – you mark off what you have already covered in the list.

Second, it will help you evaluate any textbook you may plan to purchase. By opening the book and comparing your list with the topic headings in the table of contents you will be able to determine how well the textbook covers the language's grammar.

Third, the list will tell you the order in which grammar topics should be arranged for step-by-step learning. You can try to note which items are important to you at the beginning stage, the intermediate stage, and the advanced stage of language study.

Fourth, if you are studying a rare language and you haven't been able to find a good study aid for it, you can create your own textbook from various sources. Your list of grammar topics will be the foundation for your textbook.

Summary: A list of grammar rules is an optional, but helpful, way to structure information about a foreign language concept as important as grammar. It will assist you in creating a more efficient study system.

1.9 ELECTRONIC BOOKS

Electronic books (digital versions of printed books) form a rather young direction for the book industry. The first electronic books (e-books) were created at the beginning of the 1980s. The founder of the movement is considered to be Michael Hart, creator of Project Gutenberg, the first project dedicated to electronic books.

The United States holds the leading position in the adoption of electronic books in everyday life. This segment already accounts for roughly 20% of all book production (as of 2013) in the US. This figure is significantly lower in other countries, but sales of e-book reading electronic books are nevertheless growing forcefully, signaling that this direction has great promise.

In terms of their content, electronic books are no different than printed books. They can certainly also be used to study a foreign language. Moreover, electronic books possess a number of new properties unavailable in traditional printed publications.

For example, several devices for reading electronic books have a built-in dictionary for context-sensitive translation. This is very convenient when working with books and texts that contain a lot of unfamiliar words. Looking up the meaning of new words takes only a few seconds, whereas with a paper dictionary it wouldn't be as quick.

One limitation of the built-in dictionary feature is that it is generally only available for the most popular languages: English, French, Spanish, German, Italian, etc...

Another modern technology, speech synthesis (text-to-speech), is also applicable to electronic books. It lets you listen to any text, actually transforming a literary work into an audiobook. In truth, the technology is currently still very far from perfection, so you should allow for several inaccuracies and flaws in the pronunciation.

Another tangible advantage of these digital technologies is the ability to create an enormous library of electronic books using a single reading device. Your books will be conveniently organized in this digital library, giving you easy access to any of them. Many book readers are sold pre-loaded with free books, mostly classic novels.

Electronic books are created in various formats, i.e. mobipocket, PDF, ePub, etc., which makes it possible to make a nearly exact copy of the printed publication. The technology is constantly being developed and there are already very interesting solutions that combine text, audio, and video.

An electronic book doesn't have to be limited to text alone. It can also contain color pictures, tables, diagrams, and maps. This allows publishers to create high-quality, full-fledged textbooks in digital form. Very soon there will be electronic study aids that will replace traditional printed materials because of these more advanced ways of visualizing information.

The process of studying electronic books is no different than that for traditional printed books. You read the text, write down unfamiliar words in your notebook for new words (together with the translation, if you have a contextual dictionary). Then you memorize them and review them. It's helpful to periodically re-read your book to see the recently learned words in context one more time.

You can use a book reader to take advantage of one more supplemental resource – subtitles for foreign films. Subtitles in electronic form are nearly the same thing as an electronic book. You can also read them, copy down unfamiliar words, and by so doing augment your vocabulary with living, conversational language. You can find many resources on the Internet which offer subtitles in several languages of the world.

Summary: An electronic book is one of the most modern tools that can be fully employed in the study of foreign languages. They possess a number of technological properties that are unavailable in traditional printed publications.

PRINTED MATERIALS

Part 2

This chapter considers ways to effectively use periodicals – newspapers and magazines. It will also help you become familiar with secondary forms of printed materials that can be employed in the learning process to obtain country-specific information and a deeper immersion in the foreign language.

2.1 NEWSPAPERS AND MAGAZINES

Everyone who studies a foreign language dreams being able to read real foreign newspapers and magazines as soon as possible. But in order to freely read these materials, you must have a rather good knowledge of grammar and a vocabulary of approximately 10,000 words.

For people who are just beginning language study, newspapers and magazines will be a collection of unintelligible symbols, especially if the text is in a language that uses a different writing system (for example, the Russian language for a German speaker, or the Chinese language for a French speaker). If your language of study is similar to your native language, then it will be much easier for you. However, you still shouldn't use foreign mass media resources at the beginning stage of your study.

Traditional (printed) newspapers are gradually becoming a thing of the past. Today newspapers are operating online with increasing frequency. This trend is unstoppable, and the majority of these publications will most likely soon cease to exist in printed form. That's too bad, because leafing through a "real" paper newspaper has its own inimitable charm. It wasn't long ago at all that someone sipping a cup of coffee while reading the news in a cafe represented tranquility, a steady way of life, and peace in the world.

But the world doesn't stand still. And the new technologies have their advantages. The modern man or woman has learned to take in a huge amount of information in a short period of time. A tablet computer with Internet access can replace dozens of newspapers and make it possible to find the specific information someone is interested in at a particular moment in time. Thus, in this section when we say "newspaper" we mean the printed publication and assume that the same actions can be applied to its electronic counterpart.

We have already stated that reading foreign newspapers and magazines requires considerable linguistic training. If you still have a big desire to try a newspaper at the very beginning of your study, then one of the few useful things you can do is build your vocabulary related to a specific topic.

By this we mean selecting some subject, for example, soccer, and finding a series of articles on this topic. Then try to translate as many of the words as possible in the chosen texts. There can't be an unlimited set of words related to soccer. Most likely, in each article you will encounter the words "goal", "goalkeeper", "corner kick", "coach", etc. These aren't the most important words in life, but they are great for practice and to fine-tune your personal method of working with original texts and new words.

Each person can pick a subject according to his or her personal interests: cooking, scuba diving, cars, dogs, etc. If your language study is somehow connected to your job, then perhaps it would make sense to begin with relevant professional textual materials.

You write down any new words in your notebook for new words or immediately enter them into your unified word database. After finding the meaning of a word in the dictionary and take steps to memorize it, you should read the article again after a while. In general, old materials should be periodically checked and reviewed. You are quite likely to discover something new for yourself with each reading.

Summary: Foreign newspapers and magazines are more beneficial at the intermediate and advanced stages of language study. At the beginning stage you can try to apply the technique of building your vocabulary on a specific topic.

2.2 PRINTOUTS FROM THE INTERNET

Printouts from the Internet are a type of printed materials that you create yourself for your study of a foreign language. It may not be the most advanced method – it's a combination of modern technologies with classic educational materials. Nevertheless, in certain instances it is entirely justified. Different people take in information in different ways from a computer screen or printed materials. The first approach may be better for one person, while the second may be better for another. Thus, for many people, text printed from the Internet will be regular, fully-acceptable study material.

Whenever you work with paper documents, proper organization is important. If you collect all of your printouts in the same folder, then you will end up with an excellent file of educational texts. And you don't need to be afraid of writing right on the pages of this "book".

The selection of materials to print out is another matter, which must be considered carefully. Each person can choose an area he or she is interested in, but there are certain universal categories of online information that are suitable for all. First of all, there are current events. It might be preferable to avoid especially terrible events, but this is a matter of personal taste. Major events are covered by the press throughout the day, constantly being updated with new details and revisions. By printing several articles related to the same event, you may end up with a full detective story in your hands.

It may also be helpful to follow some national issue or some important activity. For the modern student of a foreign language, knowledge of words related to politics, public administration, and global warming are a must. The Internet is always full of a slew of articles and new coverage on these topics. Not as captivating as current events, but useful nevertheless.

Some people may be interested in a selection of articles about a famous singer, athlete, or actor. Keep in mind that in this case the set of words used will be unpredictable, because reporters try to cover the broadest spectrum of the lives of public figures, including everything from the best to the worst about them.

Studying with texts from the Internet is similar to working with other printed materials. You read, underline unfamiliar words, and find their meaning in a dictionary. If you do everything properly, you then enter the new words into your unified word database and read the articles again several times in the course of a year. When your printouts are properly organized, this won't be hard to do at all.

We recommend that you also store the selected articles in electronic form. This is not mandatory, but since it doesn't require any special effort, you can do it as well.

Summary: Texts from the Internet will be convenient for those who are used to working with printed materials. They let you create a unique selection of texts on subjects that interest you.

2.3 PHRASEBOOKS

Tourist phrasebooks form a category of publications that relate to foreign language but which were not designed specifically for study purposes. The main goal of a phrasebook is to help a tourist in a difficult situation to use words to express his or her need.

Phrasebooks are most frequently divided into topics related to the daily activities of somebody on a foreign trip, for example, airport, restaurant, and hotel. Each topic contains a certain number of standard phrases and clichés that are typically used when talking to service personnel, salespeople, or strangers.

Sometimes a phrasebook will not only give phrases for the tourist to use, but the responses to them as well. The probability that the person you are talking to will respond exactly as indicated in the phrasebook is minimal, so this information is mostly suitable just for expanding your horizons and for self-education.

Despite their drawbacks when it comes to serious language study, phrasebooks can be used as a study aid. You need only pick the right book and master a few simple techniques.

In order to benefit from a phrasebook, you should find one that includes the following:

- Brief, understandable phrases. It's best if they consist of 5-7 words, no more. You can certainly memorize sentences like this.
- A transcription in your native language. It won't be very exact and will only give you an approximation of how words are read. Note that there is no transcription that reflects the correct pronunciation with 100% accuracy. Only hearing will help you learn how to speak correctly.
- A topical dictionary. It can be quite small; 300-500 words is entire adequate. Such a dictionary will most likely include the most important words of the language, which are frequently used in conversational speech.
- Country-specific information. This isn't required, but it is very useful, because it introduces variety into the learning process and lets you become familiar with the culture and customs of the country you are interested in.
- Ideally, the book will include an audio recording of its phrases and the words in the topical dictionary. Such a recording will prove invaluable when you try to master unfamiliar sounds and practice correct intonation.

Remember that a phrasebook for help on a trip abroad; it is not a study aid. It won't include instructions for use or teacher recommendations. You will have to make up the entire learning process using this kind of book.

You'll benefit the most from a phrasebook while traveling. Phrasebooks are typically short, compact publications that can be conveniently carried around on any trip, on a tour, or simply while walking around town. Being abroad will provide the best immersion in a foreign language, which will bolster your desire for learning and stimulate your memory.

While you are on a trip abroad, we recommend taking a look at the assortment of phrasebooks available at a bookstore in the city where you are staying. You will probably be able to find a great book from a local publisher.

Phrasebooks that you buy within a country will have a distinguishing feature. These reference books are very often not created by native speakers, so they sometimes use literary phrases, rather than conversational, as examples. You will be sure to understand them, but if you want to seriously study a language, it would be better to have an aid that gives examples from real life.

Keep in mind that a phrasebook should not be your primary textbook. Without an understanding of the basic elements of grammar, learning sentences turns into a mechanical process. If you don't understand why a phrase is constructed in a particular way, you won't be likely to remember it for long. Even if you begin with a phrasebook, you need to immediately start becoming familiar with grammar and the basic rules concerning nouns, verbs, articles, prepositions, etc.

In any event, memorizing words using a phrasebook will be helpful, but real success in studying a language will only come when you have a system. Then you will have created a study plan and will understand how to evaluate your progress.

The main actions involved in working with a phrasebook are the same as with any other study aid:

- Copy all of the unfamiliar words and phrases into your notebook for new words. This is a step-by-step process – you don't need to spend several hours to copy everything all at once.
- Learn the new words using a number of mnemonic techniques. Occasionally review the new words.
- Listen to the audio recording, if there is one. This exercise will be very helpful for reviewing the learned material.
- Repeat the words after the speaker. This will help you practice the correct pronunciation and intonation. It promotes better retention of the words.
- Review the words directly using the phrasebook (table-based approach). Words in a phrasebook are typically presented in three columns: the source word, the translation, and the transcription. By hiding one of the columns you can change the purpose of the review – from recalling the translation from your native language into the foreign language, or vice versa.

Since phrasebooks are usually short publications, you will spend little time mastering the whole book. For example, you might do this while you are on a trip abroad. In any event, two weeks will be sufficient to memorize the most important words and phrases.

If you feel that a phrasebook is an appropriate option for you, then, in addition to printed publications, you can find a large body of similar information on the Internet. Phrasebooks are very often provided on travel agency websites.

Summary: Tourist phrasebooks help you memorize a certain number of the most essential, frequently-used phrases. Sometimes these books include topical dictionaries that can be used to form a basic vocabulary.

2.4 TOURIST GUIDEBOOKS

Although this type of publication isn't related to linguistics, guidebooks can be helpful to expand your knowledge of a country where the language you are studying is spoken. Guidebooks often contain interesting information about the nation's history, population, religions, customs, and the peculiarities of the national cuisine. These publications can introduce you to all the important events that have happened in the country, and its national holidays and famous people.

Guidebooks are written first of all for tourists, so the bulk of their content is dedicated to tourist locations and historical monuments. If you're studying a foreign language, this information will be both interesting and beneficial to you. A guidebook may give you a multitude of geographic names that are currently mere abstractions to you, but which after reading about them will be transformed into specific concepts with enduring associations.

You will frequently encounter the names of cities, mountains, rivers, and other geographic features in your studies. You will soon constantly run into these words on the Internet, while watching foreign news, and listening to foreign radio. Your understanding of this information will be much higher if you are prepared for it.

Interesting material is easily remembered, so working with a guidebook won't take a lot of energy from you. It's more like spending your time wisely on a beneficial-but-fun pastime. A guidebook will really shine on a trip abroad, because much what you read about you will see with your own eyes.

Often these publications contain topical dictionaries and phrasebooks. These sections will be very small, but you may find them relevant at the beginning stage. Sometimes in guidebooks you can find a good explanation of how to read and information about the peculiarities of pronunciation.

When you are in a country where the language you are studying is spoken, we recommend that you drop in at an ordinary bookstore and check out its selection of guidebooks issued by local publishers. A good guidebook in a foreign language will be both an excellent souvenir and a suitable study aid.

Summary: Tourist guidebooks are a source of useful, country-specific information. Guidebooks in a foreign language can be used as a full-fledged learning aid. These publications frequently contain small topical dictionaries and phrasebooks.

2.5 MAPS AND ATLASES

These are another source of useful reference information. Having a good idea of where the country you are interested in is located, who its neighbors are, what seas surround it, etc. will only accelerate your familiarization with the nation and its language. If you aren't planning a road trip around the country, you don't need to buy highly-detailed, expensive atlases. A small foldable map or a guidebook that includes a map should be adequate. It's best if all of the geographical names are translated into two languages: your native language and the foreign language you are studying.

Frequently toponyms – the names of cities, rivers, mountains – include specific concepts, which are very interesting to discover and decipher. These words can say a lot about the history of a country, and about specific regions and cities.

Here are some examples of toponyms in several languages:

- Berg (mountain, German: Königs<u>berg</u>, Nürn<u>berg</u>)
- Ford (crossing, English: Ox<u>ford</u>, Brad<u>ford</u>)
- 川 (river, Japanese: 大川 O<u>gawa</u>, 神奈川 Kana<u>gawa</u>)

To a certain degree toponyms will help you augment your vocabulary. There aren't a lot of these words, but you will remember them for the rest of your life.

A public transportation guide, which you can purchase at a local bookstore while on a trip abroad, is an excellent, useful souvenir. This is typically a very compact publication with a great, detailed map of the city. These references books contain the most reliable information and are a part of "real life" in the country. In the same bookstore you might ask for geography textbooks designed for 10-14 year-old students. Such books will be written in simple, easy-to-understand language. You will probably glean a great many essential words from them and all kinds of interesting information.

Summary: Maps, atlases, and other literature related to geography will help you become more familiar with the country in which the language you are studying is spoken. They make great, useful souvenirs that you can bring home with you from your trip.

2.6 PRINTED SOUVENIRS

Continuing the theme of useful materials that you can find on a trip abroad, let's say a little about printed souvenirs. By this term we mean various pamphlets, postcards, newspapers, etc. that are distributed for free at hotels, airports, and tourist locations.

In developed countries where competition in sales is especially strong, manufacturers and salespeople take several measures to promote their wares. They print a large number of advertising materials that you will encounter during your trip.

You can find a lot of interesting reference books and small guidebooks at tourist information centers, travel agencies, and the offices of companies that organize city tours. Restaurant shills can also supply you with a complete arsenal of every imaginable pamphlet, flyer, and business card.

None of these materials plays a special role in the process of learning a language, but they can still prove useful. You are entirely like to see words in these advertisements that you should enter into your word database. The fact that you saw them on "real" foreign pamphlets is sure to keep them in your memory.

You can be sure that when you take a look at this collection of printed souvenirs several months after your trip that most of it will no longer be just colorful pieces of paper with unintelligible letters. You will be able read many of them freely, and that will give you confidence that you are really making progress in your language study.

Summary: While on a trip abroad you may encounter a large number of advertising pamphlets, postcards, and other materials. The most interesting of these will become great souvenirs and, most likely, a source of new useful words.

TELEVISION AND DVDS

Using television and other video materials enhances, varies, and significantly accelerates the process of learning a foreign language. This chapter describes several video resources that are reasonable to include in your study program. You can also find information here on how to choose foreign films that are most appropriate for the purpose of learning.

3.1 FOREIGN TELEVISION

By foreign television we mean any national television broadcasting channel. For example, in France there are TF1, TF2, Canal+; in Italy – RAI channels; in Poland – TVP Polonia; etc. These are TV channels that transmit news, movies, talk shows, and various other broadcasts.

A feature of television as a learning resource is its "one-timeness". In other words, you should expect that you will only be able to watch a particular broadcast or news release once. Of course, you can record a broadcast to a DVD, but in this section we will examine the use of live foreign TV, e.g. without recording to a storage device.

First, you need to determine what level of access (short-term or permanent) you have to foreign television. For example, if you're on a short tourist trip, you have short-term access. In this case, you should consider this resource as entertainment and not establish a learning goal for yourself.

The most useful thing you can do is listen to the intonation and try to repeat the speaker's pronunciation. But in general this sort of television can be "background" for you, helping you immerse yourself a bit deeper in the foreign culture. At the beginning stage watching foreign television broadcasts will simply be a distant goal – a graphic example of what you'll be able to easily understand if you work diligently to learn the language. This extra stimulus never hurt anybody.

Permanent access to foreign television will allow you to use this resource very effectively. First, you can follow interesting feature films and documentaries, thanks to announcements and a schedule of future broadcasts. Second, by selecting several regular television programs, especially news programs, you will stay informed about what is going on in the other country. Third, some broadcasts have news tickers. You should try to read them, write down unfamiliar words, and look up their meaning in the dictionary.

If you have the ability to record an interesting movie being broadcast on a foreign channel, then you can get great material for more in-depth study. You can learn how to use foreign films most effectively in the next chapter.

Summary: Viewing foreign television broadcasts is most interesting at the intermediate and advanced stages of learning. This resource will help you become more familiar with the culture of the country in which the language you are studying is spoken.

3.2 MOVIES AND SHOWS ON DVD

Modern movies and shows on DVD are an excellent learning tool for people trying to master a foreign language. In order to effectively use this resource you take several simple steps: select an appropriate collection of films and shows; find subtitles; create a word database, if you haven't already; and set aside some free time for intense study.

First, a few words about choosing films and shows. If you're interested in a popular language such as French, German or Spanish, your options will be rather broad. For less widespread languages, however, the assortment available will be much smaller.

A movie or show should be selected based on the following criteria: genre, language, subtitles, the country where it was made, and the number of episodes.

Television serials, situational comedies (sitcoms), and detective serials are the best for learning a language. Examples of these are famous series such as "Friends", "The Big Bang Theory", and "Columbo". You can probably find these serials in the language you need.

In theory, you can use any movie or show, but the categories mentioned above are the most suitable for learning a language. Sitcoms are 100% dialog and there is non-stop action. There are no long pauses, musical interludes, etc. Moreover, the dialog consists of lively conversational speech that is used in everyday life. That is, the show's characters speak exactly like people speak in real life.

Any other type of show will have a substantially smaller amount of useful dialog than sitcoms and detective serials. However, movies such as "Die Hard" may be used well for educational purposes. In general, a movie or show from any genre may be appropriate if it has enough conversational speech.

Selecting movies and shows. Audio track

Ideally, you would get a DVD movie or show that has audio tracks in two languages – the foreign language you are studying and your native language. This option would let you learn most effectively. First, you watch the movie or show in your native language and understand all of its plot's subtleties. Then you watch for learning in the foreign language.

Buying a movie or show only in the original language is good as well, but you may need to watch it a few times to understand the gist of what is going on.

It's entirely possible that the movie or show will have an audio track in some language that you know, but which is not your native language. This isn't a bad option either. You can brush up on that language at the same time you learn a new one.

Selecting movies and shows. Subtitles

In order to realize its full learning potential, a movie or show should have subtitles in the foreign language. Subtitles are needed for studying a language, because together with the audio track, they are the most important educational aspect of watching a movie or show. If you can make a printout of the subtitles, then your work will be easier. This possibility is described in more detail in the corresponding section.

Comments: Subtitles are text that accompanies video, repeating or supplementing the audio in a movie or show. More often than not subtitles reflect what characters are saying, but sometimes they contain additional information about what is happening on the screen, i.e. film commentary or explanations of places that are difficult to understand.

Selecting movies and shows. Country where it was made

When choosing a movie or show, keep in mind that in the original language they are nearly always more difficult in terms of vocabulary than movies and shows that have been translated. For example, a film originally produced in France will have authentic French in it, but at the same time it will abound with complex turns of speech and idioms.

Additionally, a French translation of the American series "Friends" will be much easier to understand, although the translation won't always reflect the beauty of the French language. Conversely, only an original French show can convey the true character of the French, and the particulars of their culture and everyday life.

Viewing a movie or show for learning

Educational viewing is a full set of actions that includes the following:

- initial, complete viewing of the movie or show
- subsequent step-by-step viewing with pauses to write down unfamiliar words and phrases
- lookup meanings of words in the dictionary
- work to learn new words and word combinations
- repetitive viewing of the movie or show
- review of the new words related to the movie or show

You can also record the audio track with an audio recording device and listen to it periodically (see the heading entitled "Audio tracks to movies and shows").

Note that watching a movie or show with frequent pauses to write down new words is an important but rather exhausting process. Therefore we recommend limiting it in terms of time (20-30 minutes) or number of words written down (30-50 words). Having the subtitles in printed form will significantly accelerate this process, because you only need to underline the unfamiliar word on the printout and only occasionally pause the movie or show.

Remember that the more carefully you choose your learning materials, the easier it will be for you to work with them and the better the result. The ideal scenario might be as follows: you have an interesting series in two languages, two sets of subtitles, and a separate audio file with the foreign language audio track.

You spend one hour a day working with the show – watching, looking up the meaning of new words, memorizing them, and reviewing them. Within 2-3 months you will develop a multitude of useful language skills and form a unique vocabulary, much of which will be firmly fixed in your memory.

Summary: Movies and shows on DVD are a fantastic learning tool for people learning a foreign language. With the right approach, this resource can produce impressive results.

3.3 EDUCATIONAL SITCOMS

There is another type of video material of interest to those beginning to study a foreign language. Educational sitcoms are short TV series that are often like the situational comedy genre.

The development of television constantly expands television's relevance. This medium's ability to affect broad segments of the population is employed for advertising, educational, and various political purposes. Experts developing study aids for learning a foreign language have also added this resource to their arsenal.

Several attempts have been made in different countries to create completely educational movies and shows. For example, the EXTR@ series, the Follow Me! English course, or the animated children's educational MUZZY videos, which, incidentally, have received a large number of international awards. We discuss each of these works briefly below.

How effective are these materials when learning a language? Generally speaking, these sitcoms can be beneficial as supplementary, secondary resource – not as a study aid, but as a tool to bolster interest in learning the language. They are particularly appropriate if you are teaching a language to your child, because most of these sitcoms are designed for children.

These sitcoms can teach a child to better understand foreign speech, and hear and remember a certain number of new words. But most importantly, the child will become familiar with a foreign culture, perceive another nation not as something abstract but as ordinary people who simply speak a different language.

Educational sitcoms can be compared with adapted books. If regular films have an arbitrary selection of words, educational sitcoms contain only words that are frequently used in conversational speech. Moreover, the construction of sentences will grow more complicated gradually from one episode to the next.

A brief description of several worthwhile educational video aids is given below. These aids are available for a limited number of languages, but you will probably be able to find similar movies and shows for learning the foreign language that you are studying.

EXTR@ series

EXTR@ is a British educational sitcom. It was produced by the Channel 4 (Great Britain) television channel from 2002 to 2004. It is considered one of the best modern series in this genre. The educational material is presented as a comedy series. Versions have been released in English, German, French, and Spanish.

Follow Me! language course

Follow Me! is a television series produced by BBC at the beginning of the 1980s. The course is designed for those studying the English language and remains highly popular to this day. It is produced as a full-fledged learning aid. The set includes books and a large number of video discs. The British actor Francis Matthews's superb performance has contributed significantly to the course's popularity.

Muzzy animated series

Muzzy is an animated, televised English-language course for children. It was also developed by BBC. The first episodes appeared in 1986. The cartoon was originally designed for children learning English. Thanks to its huge popularity, after a while versions were created for German, Spanish, French, Italian, Chinese, and Russian.

Summary: Educational sitcoms are a great supplementary resource for the beginning and intermediate levels of learning a language. They help maintain interest in learning, promote deeper immersion in the foreign language, and introduce the culture of other countries.

3.4 EURONEWS, BBC

Among the wide variety of television channels, a small group can be identified that is of particular interest to people studying a foreign language. It consists of the multilingual news channels BBC and Euronews.

Remember that foreign television and radio are most appropriate for use at the intermediate and advanced stages of learning. The main goal is to practice your ability to understand foreign speech. At the beginning stage of learning, foreign television may serve as part of your immersion in another linguistic environment and as a source of country-specific information.

BBC (British Broadcasting Corporation)

BBC is one of the largest media companies in the world. It was founded in 1922. It includes several divisions: television, radio, and Internet. BBC's worldwide service broadcasts in 28 languages. Over the course of the past decade the list of services has changed continually for various economic reasons.

As of October 2012, the following languages were supported: English, Arabic, Azerbaijani, Bengali, Burmese, Chinese, French, Hausa (Western Africa), Indonesian, Rwandese, Kirundi, Kirghiz, Nepalese, Pashto (an Afghan language), Persian, Portuguese, Russian, Sinhalese, Somali, Spanish, Swahili, Tamil, Turkish, Ukrainian, Urdu, Uzbek, and Vietnamese.

Those studying the English language will be interested in the free courses, lessons, and reference materials available in the LEARNING ENGLISH section of www.bbc.com. It includes useful, country-specific information about English-speaking nations.

EURONEWS

Founded in 1992, Euronews is a rather young company. Euronews performs round-the-clock television broadcasting in 11 languages: English, French, German, Italian, Spanish, Portuguese, Turkish, Polish, Ukrainian, Russian, Arabic, and Persian.

Euronews releases news segments every half hour. Each news item is repeated in several segments. This gives you a fantastic opportunity to hear the very same text multiple times and understand difficult words and phrases that you may have missed in the previous segments.

In addition to coverage of global events, there are a number of themed shows dedicated to scientific development, environmental protection, and various cultural events.

Euronews's satellite broadcasting lets you easily switch from one language to another. If one of these is your native language or a language that you know well, you can listen to the news in that language first and then switch to the language you are studying. Thanks to simultaneous transmission, the broadcasts in each language happen at the same time.

Summary: Multilingual television channels are a great learning resource to practice your ability to understand foreign speech. They will help you stay informed about what is going on in the country you are interested in.

RADIO. AUDIO MATERIALS

When it comes to practicing understanding foreign speech, you can't do without high-quality audio learning materials. This chapter will tell you which stages of learning are appropriate for using live radio and other audio sources. Considerable attention is given to using audio to review new words and create your own audio dictionary.

4.1 FOREIGN RADIO STATIONS

Foreign radio stations broadcasting in the language you are studying can be employed at the intermediate and advanced stages of learning to improve comprehension of foreign speech. For novices, foreign radio will prove ineffective, because the ability to comprehend rapid, conversational speech is not strong enough at the beginning stage. Foreign radio is more like a goal to strive for than a method to learn the language. Nevertheless, listening to the radio in a foreign language is worthwhile, even without great abilities.

At any stage, this will be entertaining listening. Beginners can try to recognize familiar words and make note of the intonation and overall melody of the language. Listening to foreign radio station broadcasts will undoubtedly be more beneficial to those who we might call "advanced users."

In addition to radio allowing you to practice being able to comprehend foreign speech, it is also an appropriate way to mentally refresh some of your vocabulary. News broadcasts provide useful, country-specific information and, in general, radio is an excellent way to become further immersed in the foreign language.

Try to make listening to the radio a brief morning– or evening ritual. Turn on the radio to wake yourself up or listen to a news segment before going to bed. These will prove to be very useful habits. You can also listen to the radio in the background while you do household chores. This listening is purely for entertainment, but it can bear fruit of its own. You may occasionally pick up familiar words and geographical names.

Summary: Foreign radio stations are a great learning resource, but only if you can already sufficiently understand foreign speech. Nearly every radio station has two forms of broadcasting: traditional over-the-air broadcasting and Internet broadcasting (online radio).

4.2 AUDIOBOOKS

Audiobooks, like other audio materials for learning a foreign language, are most beneficial if you can read what you are listening to. This is especially relevant at the beginning stage of learning.

Sound alone can be used for the intermediate and advanced stages, but even then it's helpful to have the full text of the audio recording. Then you can clearly see the words you don't understand, and you can look them up in the dictionary. This is a must for beginners. When choosing an audiobook at the store, it should be a set consisting of a "printed book and CD" or an "e-book with audio".

When working with an audiobook, the learning process is no different than when working with printed books. You listen to the audio, read the text, and write down unfamiliar words and phrases in your notebook for new words. Then find the meaning of the words in the dictionary, learn them, and review them.

An audiobook is great for reviewing new words and fixing them firm in your memory. Listening to books multiple times can help you remember whole sentences. You can also repeat the text after the speaker to practice your pronunciation and the intonation of phrases.

Short literary works, especially detective stories, are the best to use a learning material. They read easily and contain an excellent collection of modern words. You shouldn't try listening to historical novels at the beginning stage of learning. You'll run into a large number of obsolete concepts and other difficult-to-understand words.

Summary: Audiobooks are very useful to practice your ability to understand foreign speech. You should absolutely have the full text of the audiobook.

4.3 CAR STEREO

For people who spend a lot of time behind the wheel of a car, it would be irrational to not use the car stereo for foreign language learning. Modern sound systems support playback of CDs with recordings in various formats: MP3, WMA, FLAC, WAV, AAC, MPEG4, etc. Some car stereos have a USB port, which makes it possible to listen to songs and texts straight from a flash drive.

Driving places certain limits on the actions of the driver, whose attention is focused on the road. Therefore audio recordings must not distract the driver – they should only be in the background. When it comes to learning a language, you should choose audio materials that provide entertaining and relaxing listening.

For beginning students and inexperienced drivers, we recommend only using songs in the language being studied. This doesn't particularly help with mastering a language, but neither does it distract the driver from the road. More experienced drivers can take full advantage of the opportunities provided by free time behind the steering wheel.

There are language courses available which have been specially developed for listening to in a car. These are likely to be acceptable study aids, although the publishers often overstate their benefits. The most you can expect to gain is to somewhat improve your understanding of foreign speech and remember some words you encounter during the course. They won't help you "learn a language in 3 weeks" or "learn to speak in 1 day."

In addition to specialized audio courses, other listening material includes audiobooks, audio recordings of movies or shows, songs, radio dramas, recordings of new words, and audio dictionaries. Ideally, you will listen to the material that is part of your language study plan. For example, if you're actively following some television series, then the show's audio track on CD would be the best for the car.

Your car stereo works well for reviewing new words. If you create your own audio dictionary, you will be able to review new words more often and, consequently, have better recall. You can find information on how to create an audio dictionary in the corresponding chapter.

Summary: A car stereo is a secondary resource that can be used with success to study a foreign language. It allows you to listen to audiobooks, review words, etc. One type of listening material is an audio recording of some movie or show.

4.4. AUDIO DICTIONARIES

Audio dictionaries form their own category of language learning materials. These study aids are designed to review and reinforce foreign words, although dictionary authors may ascribe additional properties to them.

Audio dictionaries are most often intended for the beginning level of study and contain from 3,000 to 5,000 words. Words may be organized alphabetically, frequency of use, or topically.

An audio dictionary will be particularly helpful if a printed book is included with the recording. This combination forms a dictionary audiobook that you can use to see how words are spelled and check their meaning.

Comments: In this book we will use the following terms to define elements of a dictionary:
- source word – a word in your native language
- translation – the foreign word that corresponds to the source word

---

The audio material of these dictionaries may differ in the order of the translation and source word. The most common combination is "source word + translation." Ideally, you should be able to listen to an audio dictionary in 4 ways:

- foreign translation alone
- source word + translation
- translation + source word
- translation + source word + translation

Each of these combinations has its own way of helping you to memorize and review words.

For example, only listening to the foreign translation takes far less time. This means you could review your entire vocabulary in a short period of time.

The basic "source word + translation" combination is actually the most difficult. It will show you how well you remember words.

The "translation + source word" option is somewhat easier and will help you quickly recall the meaning of foreign words, which is critical to understanding foreign speech. This will also be very helpful in improving your reading skills.

Audio dictionaries implemented as computer programs offer even more opportunities. In addition to letting you select the listening combination, they allow you to control the interval between word sets. At the beginning stage you might work with a large interval in order to have enough time to recall the words. But at the advanced stage you could reduce the interval to a minimum so as to accelerate the process and listen to the entire list of words in a short time.

Your own audio dictionary

Try to create your own audio dictionary that includes all of your new words. Such a word list will let you memorize new vocabulary words faster and evaluate how well you can remember the material. Even the process of making the recording is beneficial, because any action with the words (reading, listening, enunciating) will serve to reinforce them in your long-term memory.

We recommend that you record new words in small batches. For example, suppose you found 30 new words while reading a chapter of a book. This list could become a single recording. This will make it easier for you to organize your audio files for subsequent use. You will need a computer and a microphone to make a recording. This approach will give you the best quality sound. You can also try making a recording using a dictaphone, MP3 player, or other device with a recording function. You're making the recording for your own purposes, so the important thing is that the quality be good enough for you.

In order to make a recording on a computer, you can use standard utilities included with the operating system. These are simple programs that will let you do everything you need to with the audio.

For your purposes, recording the foreign words alone is sufficient. The interval between words should be about one second. This will be enough time for you to recall a word and, if you want, say it out loud. Entirely new words are worth reviewing several times a day. Later, an occasional review will be enough. In time you will accumulate a large audio library that cannot be played in its entirety in a single lesson. But just listening to part of it each day will be great.

Reviewing words should be taken serious. When reviewing words, your full attention should be focused on the task at hand. If you turn on a recording in the background while doing something else, the result is most like going to be nothing at all. Only serious, focused effort will produce a significant positive effect. You can make a small exception for listening to an audio dictionary in the car. We recommend that only experienced drivers use an audio dictionary, preferably on roads without heavy traffic.

Summary: An audio dictionary is a tool that can significantly accelerate your memorization of new words. You can use it to easily review all the words in your vocabulary.

4.5 RADIO DRAMAS

This genre of radio broadcasting appeared some time after the development of modern radio receivers and was especially popular in the 1940-50s. Radio dramas were carefully planned and directed. The quality of radio dramas was extremely high, because professional actors were involved.

With the appearance of television in the 1950s, radio plays lost their former popularity and substantially dropped in number. But you can currently find a multitude of high-quality productions on the Internet. Their intrinsic ambience and the stellar performance of the actors will delight you.

If you can find any radio shows in your required language, you can include them in your list of study materials. At the beginning stage, listening to these productions will yield little, but it will be an entertaining and beneficial pastime for people at the intermediate and advanced stages. You probably won't succeed in finding the text of a radio show, so you'll be left with the high-quality audio alone.

Given the large number of feature films, a diligent search for radio shows may not be necessary. But if you come across any interesting recordings, we recommend listening to them.

Summary: Classic radio shows cannot be used as a true learning tool. But for people who know the language, listening to these radio productions will become an excellent pastime.

4.5 AUDIO TRACKS TO MOVIES AND SHOWS

In the preceding chapters we mentioned the possibility of using the audio tracks to movies and shows as audio material for learning a language. Now we will examine this resource more closely.

Getting an audio file that contains the talking on a movie or show is on the list of possibilities suggested by the idea of using movies or shows as study aids. With such an audio recording you can "listen to a movie" when you don't have the ability to watch it – on a train, public transportation, in the car, etc. This won't be the primary element of the learning process, but its usefulness is difficult to overstate. In addition to improving your ability to understand foreign speech each time you listen, you will also recreate scenes from the movie in your mind, which will promote memorization of words, phrases, and whole sentences.

Here's an example. You use a foreign version of the series "Friends" as a study aid and started working with the latest episode. You watched the new show, read the subtitles, and write down and looked up the meanings of 50 new words. Now your task is to learn these words. In order to reliably remember them, you need to perform a number of standard actions and not forget to repeat the new words as often as possible. You can watch the episode a few more times, and you can substitute watching with listening to the audio track. Record the audio to your MP3 player or phone and you'll be able to review the show's new words as often as you want.

To extract the audio track from a movie or show you like, you will need a simple converter program. The Internet offers a large number of these utilities. Some cost money, while others are distributed free-of-charge. All you have to do is select the desired video file and after a few minutes the program will create an audio file from it in the format you need.

Summary: By recording the audio track of a movie or show, you will obtain a "radio drama" that will fit perfectly into your study program. This recording will help you easily review words and practice your ability to understand foreign speech.

4.7 PHONETICS AIDS

The correctness of your pronunciation is one of the measures that can be used to gauge how well you know a foreign language. Sometimes a person knows a language well and can correctly construct phrases, but doesn't consider pronunciation very important. This may be acceptable if you plan to use the language primarily for reading and correspondence. But for full communication you must try to correctly pronounce the words in the language you are studying.

This is easiest if you are studying with an instructor who is a native speaker of the language. He or she can constantly correct you, point out your weak points, and think up exercises to practice difficult sounds.

Learning correct pronunciation on your own is also realistic, if you have the appropriate study materials and a huge desire to learn. You can take advantage of specialized courses; phonetics textbooks; the Internet, with its diversity of audio- and video information; and foreign movies and shows.

Keep in mind that in order to learn how to speak correctly, your exercises must be tied specifically to speaking out loud. When practicing you will need to enunciate the sounds quite loudly, and this may impact the time and place of your studies. Ideally, you will study in a quiet place without others around.

Before you begin your studies, you should get some theoretical information about the language you will be learning. You can find a lot of useful information in Wikipedia.

For example, you can learn about the International Phonetic Alphabet (IPA), a globally-accepted system for transcription. The IPA will help you form a more accurate representation of the phonology of the language you are studying.

SIL International has developed the program IPA HELP, which you can use to listen to the phonation of all of the main sounds in the International Phonetic Alphabet. The program is available for free at http://www.sil.org/computing/ipahelp/index.htm.

As an introduction, you can also look at a few phrasebooks for your desired language. Phrasebooks almost always include a section on the rules of pronunciation, typically written in simple, accessible language.

A good phonetics aid will not only give you theory about each sound, it will also give you a large number of examples. Because phonetics are usually studied at the beginning stage, the examples and exercises will most likely be straightforward and understandable.

An important part of a phonetics aid is an audio CD or some other medium on which the contents of the books are recorded. It is preferable for the recording to be made by a native speaker of the language. This will give you the best representation of the correct pronunciation.

Summary: A phonetics aid is a very useful resource for practicing correct pronunciation and intonation. This is especially true of languages with complex sounds that are difficult to master.

OPPORTUNITIES ONLINE

Part 1

In the modern world there is no information resource more global and all-encompassing than the Internet. The worldwide web provided boundless opportunities for learning a foreign language. Text, audio-, and video materials can be effectively included in your study program. This chapter discusses the most interesting and useful Internet resources.

Chapter contents:

5.1 ONLINE VIDEO MATERIALS

If you have high-speed Internet access, a huge quantity of video resources becomes available to you, in virtually any language on the planet. We can identify several similarities between these resources that affect the degree to which they are used in learning a foreign language.

We divide all video resources into the following groups:

- Online movies and shows
- Internet TV
- News videos
- Topic-specific videos
- Music videos
- Educational videos

Almost all video materials require rather advanced language skills. This is especially true of foreign television, topic-specific videos, and movies and shows without subtitles. Those beginning to study a language will be faced with a completely unrecognizable stream of sounds, with only an occasional familiar name or place sneaking in.

We recommend spending an insignificant amount of time working with these materials at the beginning stages. The purpose of watching them will be primarily to continue to be immersed in the foreign language. Later you can establish some real learning goals for yourself.

The sole exception to this general rule is educational videos, which are usually designed for the beginning stage and provide basic information related to grammar, phonetics, and other aspects of a foreign language.

Summary: High-speed Internet access provides the ability to use another interesting resource – online video materials – to learn a language. You can benefit the most from these materials at the intermediate and advanced stages of learning.

5.2 NEWS WEBSITES

The Internet has a lot of interesting materials that can be used for educational purposes. One example of this sort of information is national news websites. These are basically electronic newspapers that contain a wide variety of columns: economics, culture, sports, current events, travel, etc.

These newspaper websites are good in that they usually consist of short articles and news stories. In other words, you can confidently use these texts for a single lesson.

If you choose to use the Internet and news websites as learning materials, then to that end you can keep a separate notebook for new words and add words to it from all the articles that you work with. In doing so, you should indicate the article heading, its source, and the date. This will let you easily find the original source and review the words in context.

Another benefit of these resources is that the words used in them are sure to be modern and relevant. That is, they will represent the "real" foreign language – the way it is used in real life, as opposed to adapted texts.

News websites have an additional advantage in that many news items are not one-time reports, but rather ongoing coverage of a story. The correspondents follow the development of the most interesting events and report new information each day. With time you might collect a large set of related articles about a particular event, which you can read like a book.

Because you have followed the story from the very beginning, you will be able to quite easily understand each subsequent news article.

Summary: News websites are one of the best sources of information on current events in the country that speaks the language you are studying. You can also use this resource to augment your vocabulary with modern, relevant words.

5.3 INDUSTRY- AND TOPIC-SPECIFIC WEBSITES

Industry-specific websites are websites dedicated to some profession. This includes websites about cars, medicine, geology, ecology, etc. They will be particularly interesting if you follow a specific area in business, culture, or sports.

Topic-specific websites are websites that contain information about any everyday human pursuits, interests, or hobbies. For example, these might include cooking websites that publish recipes and tips for preparing dishes. Another example is sites about hunting and fishing.

For some people the websites of well-known international corporations become a good resource. These enterprises spend significant funds to maintain their image and they typically represent themselves online very professionally.

Industry- and topic-specific sites may contain a great deal of specialized information and rare words, often in industry jargon. These websites will be useful at the intermediate and advanced stages of learning. You will probably find topics you are interested in on these sites. Learning a foreign language is always more productive when the instruction is based on captivating, high-quality material.

The method for working with industry- and topic-specific websites is the same as with other texts. You read the text, write down new words in your notebook, and work with the dictionary. It is desirable to occasionally re-read these texts to reinforce and review the words you've encountered recently.

Summary: Industry- and topic-specific websites will help you find texts that you specifically find interesting. These resources are most appropriate for the intermediate and advanced stages of learning.

5.4 TOPIC-SPECIFIC VIDEOS

Topic-specific videos are what we call all types of short videos, whether amateur or professional, which contain any kind of speech. For example, a presentation about a new car that describes its features in detail. Or a tourism video about an old, medieval city. The Internet has a huge number of these mini-videos about every topic imaginable. You are sure to find something fitting just for you.

For people with intermediate and advanced language skills, watching these videos will be entertaining – relaxation with benefits. These videos strengthen your ability to understand foreign speech. You may encounter a lot of familiar words, especially if you find a clip on a subject that is of interest to you.

The footage being shot specifically in the country of the language you are studying is another great plus, because it will help you better familiarize yourself with the culture of the other country and better understand the lifestyle of local residents. All of this will help bolster your interest in the culture of the other country and, as a consequence, make studying the language more meaningful and fascinating.

Topic-specific videos can also be used as a test to evaluate the adequacy of your vocabulary or the level of your understanding of foreign speech. If you watch the same video every 2-3 months, you can easily determine if you are making progress.

If you've just begun learning a language, this resource is probably not applicable due to your limited vocabulary. These videos can't play a practical educational role for beginners, because they typically don't have subtitles. That leaves the audio track, which for beginners will only be an unintelligible stream of sounds.

Summary: Topic-specific videos are short video presentations that contain a narrative about some subject, event, exotic place, etc. These videos are useful to practice your ability to understand foreign speech.

5.5 ONLINE NEWS VIDEOS

Many national search engines such as Yahoo (USA), Wanadoo (France), and Daum (Korea), have sections for news articles and a collection of news videos.

These short clips contain information about the latest events in the country and the world, and other interesting facts. They are usually brief, informative productions, but sometimes there are full-fledged TV broadcasts with news, a weather forecast, etc.

Online news videos can be considered a type of topic-specific video. The benefit of this resource is intensified by the fact that the information is new and fresh, which lets you more deeply immerse yourself in the foreign language. In terms of their suitability for learning a language, what we said about topic-specific websites applies to news videos.

The material will be in greater demand at the intermediate and advanced stages when you will at least be able to vaguely understand the meaning of the communication. In any event, news videos are useful to maintain interest in your language studies.

If you watch the news often enough, you can stay current with everything important that's happening in the country. You will get to know the names of national celebrities – politicians, culture- and science personalities – basic geographical names, and other concepts characteristic of the nation. This will be very helpful in expanding your horizons and giving you confidence when communicating with foreigners.

Summary: Online news videos are a type of topic-specific video, in which most of the stories are dedicated to the interesting events happening in a country. They are a great source of country-specific information. They are most relevant for people working on perfecting their language skills.

5.6 MUSIC VIDEOS

Music videos are a purely entertaining resource without any real potential for educational use. You can find a multitude of music videos online in any language in the world. If you want you can add them to your media library.

In order to get the maximum educational benefit from music videos you must be able to find the text for them. There are quite a few websites offering this information. Finding the text of a song in English will be much easier than, say, finding it in Czech. But it's entirely likely that you will succeed in finding something useful, even for rare languages.

If you have the video clip and the text of the song, then the learning process will be the same as for a movie with subtitles. You identify and write down unfamiliar words. Then you look up their meaning in the dictionary. After that you do the normal work to learn the new words and periodically review them.

Songs are good in that you can listen to them many times, especially if you really like them. Keep in mind that songs often use non-standard language. You will encounter slang; unusual, modern turns of speech; and very rare "poetic" words.

Summary: Music videos are a supplementary learning resource from which you derive the maximum benefit by using the standard method for working with texts: writing down and learning the unfamiliar words. Listening to songs repeatedly helps reinforce the words.

5.7 FOREIGN ONLINE STORES

You can think of foreign online stores as a type of topic-specific website. The main benefit of these informational resources lies in the fact that you can augment your vocabulary with peculiar, mundane words which are widely used in everyday communication.

Online stores can be used encyclopedic reference for the exact names of items of clothing, household appliances, and many other items for the home. These terms are frequently absent from dictionaries, because dictionaries are updated very rarely, but new technologies and inventions appear every day.

Another advantage of online stores is the images of the items. You will learn words much more quickly and confidently when you have visual support. These websites provide the image and name of an item, and often include a description which will help establish a more lasting association. In other words, they are their own sort of visual dictionary.

At the beginning stage of learning, you can use these commercial websites to build your vocabulary. At the intermediate and advanced stages, you can use them for light reading that will let you review peculiar "everyday" language.

The best online stores to choose are country-specific websites that were originally created in the language you need. This is because you may sometimes come across international sites with text that was generated using machine translation. And it is usually far from adequate.

Summary: Foreign online stores are a supplementary informational resource that you can use to augment your vocabulary with modern concepts related to home appliances, etc. The presence of images facilitates more rapid assimilation of new words.

5.8 ONLINE MOVIES AND SHOWS

Online movie rentals are gradually growing in popularity, but, despite the many advantages, for people studying a language this resource is much less compelling than movies and shows on DVD.

Many countries have special websites offering any film for a nominal subscription fee. You can find online rentals for the latest releases, popular TV series, and nature documentaries.

But if you don't have a substantial vocabulary, you will have difficulty understanding the rapid stream of words. You will only be able to catch individual words and simple phrases. And since most online shows rarely include subtitles, much of what the characters say will remain unintelligible.

As with foreign television, you should think of online movies and shows as entertainment with benefits, and not set any particular learning goals for yourself. At the intermediate and advanced stages these movies and shows will be an excellent way to practice your ability to understand foreign speech.

Remember that in order to receive the greatest benefit from foreign movies and shows you must be able to watch them multiple times. You should also have the original subtitles (preferably in printed and electronic form).

Summary: Foreign online movies and shows can be included in your foreign language study program, but only at the intermediate and advanced stages of learning.

5.9 ONLINE RADIO

In the section entitled "Foreign radio stations" we already described ways to use radio to learn a foreign language. Now we will the particulars of this method with respect to online radio.

Virtually every FM radio station in the world today broadcasts in two ways: over-the-air and online. A large number of stations broadcast exclusively online. While over-the-air transmissions are only available to listeners within the coverage zone, online broadcasts cover the entire globe.

The wide availability of online radio is an important advantage. You can use it to receive transmissions from stations anywhere in the world. At a minimum this requires a computer and a broadband, preferably unlimited, Internet connection, because significant bandwidth is consumed to receive the audio stream.

Most online radio stations transmit broadcasts in popular audio formats – usually MP3, AAC, or WMA. Moreover, you can typically choose which format you want. The audio quality depends on the bit rate (the compression level of the audio stream) used by the station to broadcast its programs over the Internet. This parameter is measured in Kbps (kilobits per second) and it signifies how many kilobits of data are being sent to the listener. The higher this figure is, the better the audio quality. For example, 128 Kbps is close to the sound of a compact disc, while the lowest quality – 24 Kbps – is more like the sound of a telephone conversation.

The Internet contains a large number of online radio stations in any language in the world. There are special websites that create lists of these radio stations, i.e. radiotuna.com, listenlive.eu, laradiofm.com, and omniglot.com. These websites let you easily choose a radio station in your required language and style. Talk radio is best for the purpose of learning a foreign language, i.e. radio stations that broadcast news, reporting, interviews, and radio dramas.

Most of the radio stations you encounter will be music stations. Songs may be included in the learning process, but to receive a noticeable result from them you will need the song lyrics and at least some semblance of a plan to use them. With the right approach, you can transform music into a useful and enjoyable study aid.

Online radio has one huge advantage that's important to people studying a foreign language. Since most online broadcasts are audio recordings, you can listen to them as many times as you want. If there is something you don't understand, you can always correct this when listening the next time. Live online broadcasts do exist, but recorded broadcasts are more interesting from an educational point of view.

Remember that radio is not an appropriate resource for beginners. We recommend that you include radio in your list of study materials after you have mastered the basic rules of grammar and attained a vocabulary of at least 3,000 words.

Summary: Online radio stations are a great resource to practice your ability to understand foreign speech. They are most effective at the intermediate and advanced stages of learning. If you are looking specifically for educational audio materials, a better choice would be audiobooks (printed book + audio recording) or specialized audio courses.

OPPORTUNITIES ONLINE

Part 2

In this chapter you will find additional information about using the Internet to learn a language – specifically about special instructional websites and educational videos. We also describe special programs called concordancers and provide examples of how to use them to work with foreign words.

Chapter contents:

6.1 INSTRUCTIONAL VIDEOS

YouTube is a wonderful resource that offers a large number of short videos dedicated to learning languages. We recommend that you adopt it as an information source and include some of the available videos in your study plan.

First you need to understand the volume of available materials and then choose the most interesting of them. As always, there will be more videos for learning English than for other languages. French, German, Italian, Spanish, and Chinese are also quite popular.

The selection is generally substantially smaller for other languages. This is good and bad. You can easily find all of the available videos, but they won't always be able to meet your needs. Short videos about pronunciation and how to read may be especially suitable to you at the beginning stage of your studies.

Keep in mind that the videos aren't always professionally made, so it can be difficult at times to judge how well the material is presented. One thing is certain – if native speakers are doing the talking in the video, then you'll hear correct pronunciation and be able fully benefit from your studying.

There is a separate category of instructional mini-videos: flash cards. You can use them online. In fact, these videos are best for practicing pronunciation, but for memorizing words you should use other resources: topical dictionaries, full-fledged computer programs, and apps like memocards.

Summary: If you find high-quality instructional videos for the language you are studying, you can include them in your study program as a supplementary tool, especially for practicing pronunciation at the beginning stage.

6.2 ONLINE LESSONS

Among websites dedicated to learning foreign languages you will encounter material presented in the form of online lessons. This will most likely be exercises for individual rules of grammar or phonetics. You won't find a complete course on a single, integrated website. By looking at several of these online resources, you will be able to form an idea of the set of useful information that you will find interesting. Just as with ordinary printed textbooks, one website might present some topics well, i.e. verbs, while another website might give an in-depth description of phonetics.

The exercises offered are similar to those provided in many traditional study aids. We will mention several of the most common standard exercises:

- multiple choice questions
- multiple choice cloze test
- open cloze test
- matching

When choosing online lessons you should pay attention to who created the website. Sites developed and maintained by language institutes or major publishers are more trustworthy. However, websites provided by individual enthusiasts may also be extremely functional and useful.

Sometimes you may discover online lessons for a foreign language on the websites of various travel agencies that are using them as a marketing tool. In this case, chances are that you're dealing with a copy of material published on some other more specialized website. You should find the original source and work with the material there.

Summary: Online lessons can be a good tool for learning a language, but you must be able to evaluate the available courses.

6.3 ONLINE DICTIONARIES

An online dictionary is a convenient Internet resource that significantly accelerates the process of translation. Good dictionaries clarify ambiguous words and provide examples on how to use them. Very often they are online versions of traditional printed publications.

The best dictionaries – both printed and electronic – come from companies like Oxford, Macmillan, Larousse, Hachette, and Langenscheidt. These are major publishers whose books have a good reputation. If you find such a dictionary in the language combination you need, you can be confident in the quality of its content.

There are also a number of excellent multilingual dictionaries, for example, wordreference.com, which offers more than 20 different dictionaries in 15 languages. Another interesting site is www.dict.cc, which lets you search for words in more than 100 language combinations.

In addition to bilingual dictionaries, i.e. English-Spanish, there are also monolingual reference books that contain a list of foreign words along with explanations in the same language. Even if your knowledge of a foreign language is small, such a resource can be very useful.

Monolingual dictionaries are generally created by national publishers or institutions, which makes these publications more trustworthy. The number of dictionary entries in these books reaches 100,000. This is enough for even the most demanding students.

Summary: Online dictionaries can become a great help in the learning process, so we recommend spending some time to find suitable dictionary resources online.

6.4 ONLINE TRANSLATORS

Online translators are a type of electronic dictionary. They are also designed for looking up the meaning of foreign words, but they typically have a smaller set of features. Most of the time these programs simply output possible translations of individual words, without any comments or examples of usage.

Despite their limitations, they can be a helpful resource. We recommend collecting and storing links to all the good online translators for your required language, so you can refer to them in the future. The tasks will be much easier for students of popular languages such as English, French, German, etc., because there is an enormous selection. You can use several tools that have an interface you like as well as good translation quality. The options available for less common languages will be small, so you will have to be content with what there is.

You can only determine how good an online translator is by using it. You will probably need several of them. One of them will become your primary resource, while the rest will be secondary. You can perform an up-front test of the programs you find. To do this you only need to choose 10 words that different in their frequency of use and then try to translate them.

When choosing a translator you should pay attention to the nationality of the tool's creator. It's best if the translator is created by a company specifically from the country of the language you are studying. But if you can't find one like that, you can try using some other translator.

In regard to the abilities of these programs to translate blocks of text, keep in mind that not one of the existing translators, even the most famous, produces a practical, high-quality translation. You can use an online translator to translate text if you simply need to understand the general meaning of an online article or an email. Under no circumstances should translations obtained this way be used as study material.

Specialized online translators that offer a single language pair (for example, French-Bulgarian and Bulgarian-French) are usually of high quality than multilingual translators. However, there are highly successful multilingual translators.

Summary: An online translator is a reference tool for translating words. Sometimes they support translating entire blocks of text. It's a good idea to find and save links to these tools at the very beginning of your studies. Each translator has a different set of capabilities and a different number of dictionary entries.

6.5 CORPORA

A corpus is all the words that make up one or more literary works. For example, there is a corpus of Bible words that contains all of the words (including prepositions, interjections, etc.) found in the Bible.

For a person studying a foreign language, national corpora are of greatest interest. These resources contain a very large number of words (often more than 100 million) and are created over the course of several decades using material from newspapers, magazines, literary works, movies and TV shows, etc. Their colossal size makes it possible to find any word that exists in a language.

We present information below about several national corpora:

Corpus of Spanish – A collection of the Spanish language

- Creator: Mark Davies, a professor of corpus linguistics at Brigham Young University
- 100 million words (sources: 20,000 Spanish texts, including television and radio programs, short stories, performances, movie scripts, newspapers and magazines, and other materials)
- It is available for use free-of-charge at http://www.corpusdelespanol.org/

This resource also offers a number of other corpora, including for English and Portuguese (Fig. 1).

KorpusDK – A corpus of the Danish language.

- Created by the company Det Danske Sprogog Litteraturselskab.
- It contains roughly 56 million words gathered from a large number of diverse sources.
- It is available for use free-of-charge at http://ordnet.dk/.

Russian National Corpus

- Creator: The Vinogradov Institute of the Russian Language and a group of linguists.
- The corpus contains approximately 150 million words from 55,000 sources.
- It is available for use free-of-charge at http://www.ruscorpora.ru/.

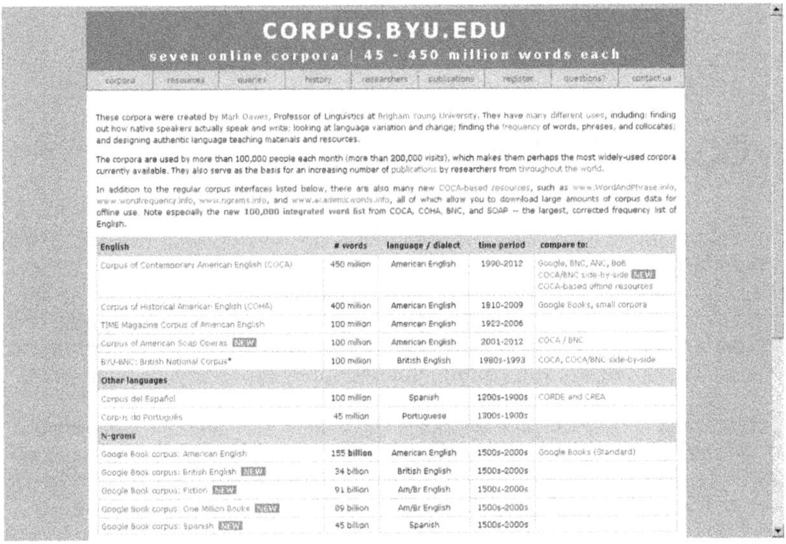

CORPUS.BYU.EDU

seven online corpora | 45 - 450 million words each

corpora | resources | queries | history | researchers | publications | register | questions? | contact us

These corpora were created by Mark Davies, Professor of Linguistics at Brigham Young University. They have many different uses, including: finding out how native speakers actually speak and write; looking at language variation and change; finding the frequency of words, phrases, and collocates; and designing authentic language teaching materials and resources.

The corpora are used by more than 100,000 people each month (more than 200,000 visits), which makes them perhaps the most widely-used corpora currently available. They also serve as the basis for an increasing number of publications by researchers from throughout the world.

In addition to the regular corpus interfaces listed below, there are also many new COCA-based resources, such as www.WordAndPhrase.info, www.wordfrequency.info, www.ngrams.info, and www.academicwords.info, all of which allow you to download large amounts of corpus data for offline use. Note especially the new 100,000 integrated word list from COCA, COHA, BNC, and SOAP -- the largest, corrected frequency list of English.

English	# words	language / dialect	time period	compare to:
Corpus of Contemporary American English (COCA)	450 million	American English	1990-2012	Google, BNC, ANC, BoE COCA/BNC side-by-side NEW COCA-based offline resources
Corpus of Historical American English (COHA)	400 million	American English	1810-2009	Google Books, small corpora
TIME Magazine Corpus of American English	100 million	American English	1923-2006	
Corpus of American Soap Operas NEW	100 million	American English	2001-2012	COCA / BNC
BYU-BNC: British National Corpus*	100 million	British English	1980s-1993	COCA, COCA/BNC side-by-side
Other languages				
Corpus del Español	100 million	Spanish	1200s-1900s	CORDE and CREA
Corpus do Português	45 million	Portuguese	1300s-1900s	
N-grams				
Google Book corpus: American English	**155 billion**	American English	1500s-2000s	Google Books (Standard)
Google Book corpus: British English NEW	34 billion	British English	1500s-2000s	
Google Book corpus: Fiction NEW	91 billion	Am/Br English	1500s-2000s	
Google Book corpus: One Million Books NEW	89 billion	Am/Br English	1500s-2000s	
Google Book corpus: Spanish NEW	45 billion	Spanish	1500s-2000s	

Fig.1 Mark Davies' corpora collection. Source http://corpus.byu.edu/

Summary: A corpus is a complete list of words from literary, musical, audio-visual, or any other work. For people studying a foreign language, national corpora will be of greatest interest.

6.6 CONCORDANCERS

Special programs called concordancers are used to work with corpora. These programs generate a list of usages of any word or phrase within a specific corpus. The resulting list of examples is usually called a concordance. The large corpora you can find on the Internet general already have an integrated concordancer capable of quickly processing an enormous body of information. The concordancer lets you perform the necessary operations with the words.

Corpora and concordancers are helpful to writers, translators, and journalists for analyzing text. In linguistics and philology they are used by university students, teachers, and the authors of foreign dictionaries. You can also derive benefit from this resource if you spend some time to learn how to use it.

When learning a language a concordancer is primarily used to determine how a given word is used. These programs also frequently support working with phrases and provide lots of results to meet your needs as accurately as possible.

An example of search results from the Danish national corpora is given below (Fig. 2). The keyword used was mandag (Monday).

Pic.2 An example of a concordance. Source: http://ordnet.dk/

Working with concordancers and corpora can be beneficial at the intermediate and advanced stages of learning. These resources are very useful when you need to clarify the nuances between synonyms or ambiguous words. A concordancer will help you find a multitude of examples of the use of prepositions, articles, verbs, and set expressions.

In addition to using prepared corpora, you can create your own word database based on one or more books, film subtitles, scientific articles, and other texts. You will end up with a unique collection of words.

We will provide one more example of using a corpus and a concordancer. Suppose that while studying you encounter a word, and no matter what you do you can't remember its meaning. Using a concordancer you can get a large number of example phrases. Two or three of them are guaranteed to be dramatic, memorable sentences. If you write these sentences down and look at them occasionally, you're chances of remembering the word increase significantly.

Another possible use of a concordancer is to create a frequency word list. Most concordancers include an option to sort the words based on their frequency of use in the text. This feature is widely used by the authors of dictionaries and other language learning aids. The more words there are in a corpus, the more representative the sorted result will be. This functionality will produce a list in which words are ordered according to how often they are used. Naturally, you might choose to learn the most common words first and then the rest. At the intermediate and advanced stages, this concordancer feature will become an opportunity for you to deliberately add new words to your vocabulary.

Summary: A concordancer is a program you can use to perform various operations on words in a particular corpus. You can create frequency lists, retrieve examples of usage of specific words, etc.

Here is a list of online resources dedicated to national corpora:

English	http://corpus.byu.edu/
	http://www.lextutor.ca/concordancers/concord_e.html
Bulgarian	http://search.dcl.bas.bg/
Dutch	http://gtb.inl.nl/
Greek	http://hnc.ilsp.gr/en/
	http://sek.edu.gr/index.php?en
Danish	http://ordnet.dk/
	http://corp.hum.sdu.dk/corpuseye.da.html
Hebrew	http://hebrewcorpus.nmelrc.org/search.php
Spanish	http://corpus.byu.edu/
Italian	http://corpora.dslo.unibo.it/coris_eng.html
	http://badip.uni-graz.at/
	http://www.vocabolario.org/
Kazakh	http://til.gov.kz/wps/portal/
Catalan	http://www.ub.edu/cccub/
Mongolian	http://web-corpora.net/MongolianCorpus/
	search/?interface_language=en
German	http://www.ids-mannheim.de/kl/projekte/korpora/
	http://www.lextutor.ca/concordancers/concord_g.html
	http://www.korpora.org/Limas/einfach.htm
Norwegian	http://corp.hum.sdu.dk/cqp.no.html
Persian (Farsi)	http://ece.ut.ac.ir/dbrg/bijankhan/
Polish	http://nkjp.pl/
Portuguese	http://corpus.byu.edu/
	http://www.corpusdoportugues.org/
Serbian	http://www.serbian-corpus.edu.rs/ns/eindex.htm
Slovenian	http://www.fidaplus.net/
Romanian	http://corp.hum.sdu.dk/cqp.ro.html
Russian	http://narusco.ru/
Turkish	http://www.tnc.org.tr/index.php/en/
Finnish	http://corp.hum.sdu.dk/cqp.sv.html
French	http://www.lextutor.ca/concordancers/concord_f.html
	http://sites.univ-provence.fr/delic/corpus/index.html
	http://corp.hum.sdu.dk/cqp.fr.html
Croatian	http://riznica.ihjj.hr/
Czech	http://ucnk.ff.cuni.cz/
Swedish	http://spraakbanken.gu.se/
Esparanto	http://corp.hum.sdu.dk/cqp.eo.html
Estonian	http://www.cl.ut.ee/korpused/segakorpus/

ELECTRONIC DEVICES

Modern technology offers a multitude of new possibilities to people learning foreign languages. This chapter examines the particulars of using various types of computers and a few other digital devices widely used in everyday life.

7.1 DESKTOP PERSONAL COMPUTERS

Desktop computers are increasingly being displaced by other personal devices: laptops, netbooks, tablets, and smartphones. But a PC offers the greatest capabilities that may be required when using a computer to learn a foreign language.

Desktop models are the most powerful and productive. More educational programs, audio editors, and other applications have been developed for desktops than for other platforms.

A desktop computer can give you everything you need to learn a foreign language, except one thing: mobility. A PC is ideally suited for people who are able to spend a lot of time at home. This type of stationary education is often far more effective than trying to learn a language on the run, on the road, or during breaks.

7.2 LAPTOPS AND NETBOOKS

There are two very similar categories of portable computers. The main difference is that netbooks are smaller and lighter than laptops. As a rule, they also have less processing power.

The term "netbook" suggests that the primary purpose of these computers is to work with the Internet. Netbooks can handle simple programs very well and are capable of running for a long time without being recharged.

Laptop computers, which are more powerful machines, have virtually the same capabilities as desktops. A good laptop computer will be sufficient to meet all of your needs. With a laptop you can read books, subtitles, and online articles; watch movies and shows; listen to the radio; and converse with native speakers using Skype.

A laptop's big advantage is its portability. This property will affect both how you organize your study time and how you store the necessary information. You won't have to copy files to a different device in order to take them with you. An accurate and uncomplicated data storage system will prove invaluable in your studies.

We recommend that you use this type of computer as your primary tool and build your learning process around it. All of the other devices (dictaphone, smartphone, tablet computer, etc.) can be great additions, but the best hub for the entire system will be a powerful, late-model laptop.

7.3 TABLET COMPUTERS

The first tablet computers appeared in the 1990s and were initially targeted at professionals. Modern tablets are highly popular among the general public and already nearly match laptops in terms of their technical specifications. There are several different categories of tablet computers: Internet tablets, laptop-tablet hybrids, and ultrabooks.

Any model of tablet computer will do for the purpose of learning a foreign language, but the set of available features and processing power can differ dramatically. The most basic tablets are more like media players in terms of their capabilities and cost. They can also be useful, but the most interesting are the more expensive and state-of-the-art models with lots of memory.

Tablet computers are ideal for reading electronic books, newspapers, and online articles. Watching movies on a tablet is also a big delight. Another educational application of such a device is listening to audiobooks and reading the recorded texts, where you read the book while the computer highlights and enunciates the phrases. A rather large number of language learning programs have already been developed for tablet computers. By taking advantage of a tablet computer's features, its portability, and its compatibility with an ordinary PC, you can make it an important element of your learning process.

7.4 MP3 PLAYERS

We will use this term to refer to the most basic mobile devices, which are primarily designed to playback audio files. These are usually tiny gadgets with either a small 2-3 line display or without one altogether. You may also see MP3 players for sale with different features (a large screen, the ability to playback video, etc.). We classify these devices as media players, which we will discuss below.

MP3 players are light and easy to use while engaged in active sports. And their low cost makes them accessible to all. These basic players are convenient for listening to audiobooks and songs in a foreign language, and reviewing words, if you have recorded your unified word database.

Many MP3 players have rather awkward navigation controls, especially models without a screen. You control them using only buttons. This makes them better for listening to files sequentially rather than frequently searching for tracks manually. On the positive side, these devices have enormous storage capacity and a long battery life. Some models of MP3 players can operate for 20 hours without a recharge.

7.5 MEDIA PLAYERS

Portable media players are a separate category of devices that stands between basic MP3 players and tablet computers. A good media player has a large color screen, a high-capacity flash drive, and an easy-to-use operating system that supports any format of media files.

Media players differ greatly in their feature sets. For those learning a foreign language, the most interesting models are true multimedia centers – they support playback of audio and video files in various formats, and they let you read electronic books, listen to the radio, and run educational apps like memocards. Some models of players have a built-in FM transmitter, which is particularly relevant when using the device in the car to broadcast the sound to a radio station on the car stereo.

There are very useful models where the integrated video player provides the necessary functionality and convenience when watching video in various formats. The user can quickly search through the video, switch between files, select an audio track, enable and disable subtitles, adjust the aspect ratio, etc. In general, these devices are becoming increasingly like tablet computers, and they can be rightfully called "mini tablets."

7.6 HANDHELD TRANSLATORS

The first electronic translators appeared in the 1990s and were a unique product in their day, carving out their own niche in the market. These devices have always been quite expensive. And at present, many models of electronic translators are comparable to laptops in price. They are essentially specialized portable computers.

The primary purpose of these devices is to translate words and phrases. But current models include lots of other useful features such as pronunciation of words, full-fledged language courses, reading of electronic books, watching videos, and much more.

When selecting a handheld translator you should carefully research each model in order to understand how well it suits you. Electronic translators usually include a wide range of dictionaries. Therefore it wouldn't at all be uncalled for to get all the information you can about the language you're interested in.

Manufacturers frequently summarize information in their product descriptions, which can confuse the consumer. For example, if it says the translator contains 3 million dictionary entries, you should understand that this is the number of words for all the languages on the device. In other words, this figure will be much smaller for each individual language. The best known brands of electronic translators are Assistant, Casio, and Ectaco. Each of these manufacturers has acquired its own unique expertise. It is this know-how that allows them to compete with other modern devices such as tablet computers and smartphones.

7.7 DICTAPHONES

While learning a foreign language you may need to record your own voice to listen to later occasionally. This might be new words or passages from books that you have included in your study program. Nowadays, making such a recording isn't difficult at all.

Dictaphones are built into many modern devices: media players, mobile phones, cameras, not to mention tablet computers and laptops. They are provide adequate quality for recording speech and can be used for the purposes indicated above. But handheld dictaphones still exist, and we'll say a few words about them.

One of the primary purposes of a handheld dictaphone is to quickly record someone else's voice. Therefore they are frequently used by journalists, students during lectures, and businesspeople during negotiations. You can also use this capability to improve your foreign language study skills.

During a trip abroad you can record the foreign speech that surrounds you: interesting television broadcasts, the voices of people speaking at the airport, and even random conversations on public transportation. Not only will these recordings become great souvenirs, they will also become original study material.

But a handheld dictaphone's greatest benefit comes when you are memorizing and reviewing foreign words. You can use it to record your current batch of new words and review them again and again until you are sure you have them perfectly memorized. A dictaphone lets you quickly record words in any order – foreign words alone or in combination with the source word.

Modern digital dictaphones can easily connect to a computer, so you can copy your recordings to or from your hard drive without any problems.

7.8 E-READERS

E-readers are devices that have truly revolutionized the book industry. Following the appearance of e-readers, printed books have begun to gradually be considered old-fashioned, and the market of familiar bookstores has undergone a fundamental shakeup. E-readers have gained wide distribution thanks to novel screen technology based on "electronic ink." The screen consumes very little energy, which allows a device to run for several weeks without being recharged.

As of today, there are a multitude of models of e-readers, and the major players in the book industry have developed their own devices, for example, Amazon (Kindle), Barnes & Noble (Nook), Sony (Sony Reader), and more.

The main purpose of an e-reader is to read electronic books. Some manufacturers have begun to equip their products with additional features, further erasing the distinction between e-readers and tablet computers. But the main purpose remains reading books, newspapers, and other texts.

Although these devices are somewhat awkward compared with other devices (slow paging turning, etc.), their low price and long battery life make them popular among a highly diverse reading audience. Someone studying a foreign language will be interested in an e-reader to read foreign books, textbooks, and to review new words. If your reader supports electronic dictionaries with contextual translation, your reading speed will increase significantly.

7.9 SMARTPHONES

A smartphone is a multi-purpose personal device capable of performing a large number of functions which previously could only have been performed by very powerful computers. All smartphones can playback of audio and video files, making them true multimedia centers.

A smartphone can be useful in studying a foreign language, but you shouldn't overestimate its possibilities. Rather the small screen size and the absence of a full keyboard make the device a supplementary entertainment device. What a smartphone can handle well is watching movies on the road, listening to audiobooks, and reviewing recorded words, e.g. the functions of a multimedia player.

Lots of specialized programs called apps have been developed for smartphones. For example, there are more than 500,000 of these apps for the iPhone. A subset of this fantastic number of programs is dedicated to learning a foreign language. You can get apps for memorizing words, learning grammar, writing lessons, and much more. All of these programs are extremely inexpensive.

Many of the small utilities may be truly useful, but this still won't be sufficient for meaningful instruction. In order to learn a language well, you must steadfastly follow your educational program, including using textbooks, printed books, audio materials, foreign movies and shows, and reference books.

METHODS AND TECHNIQUES

The ability to learn a foreign language is nothing other than possessing a broad set of specialized skills. This chapter describes several methods to reliably memorize and review foreign words. It also gives advice regarding what steps must be taken at the very beginning of your studies to form an effective study program.

Chapter contents:

8.1 PRELIMINARY PREPARATION

Unified word database

Before you begin actively studying a foreign language, we recommend that you begin a unified word database – your own personal dictionary. This can be an Excel spreadsheet or a file from some other program that can manipulate tables. You will enter into the database all of the new words you encounter from every possible source: books, movies and shows, textbooks, phrasebooks, etc. This dictionary is very convenient for reviewing and evaluating your vocabulary, and for other actions with words.

Notebook for new words

This is an intermediate repository for the new words that you will later transfer to your unified word database. You may several notebooks: one for books you are reading, another for texts from the Internet, etc. It's convenient to arrange the words in three columns: the source word, the translation, and the transcription. Spiral-bound notebooks with 100 sheets are best for this.

1,500 core words

When learning a foreign language, you can build your vocabulary slowly by reading textbooks and completing grammar exercises. But there is another way. In parallel with the standard learning process, you can make a list of the most important words of the language you are studying and try to learn them regardless of your main course. The optimum number of words in this list is roughly 1,500, but you can choose a different number at your discretion.

Transparent words

Transparent words are words that require virtually no effort to remember. Each language contains internationalisms, which are universally-accepted concepts, many of which have come from English. In his book "The Art and Science of Learning Languages", Erik Gunnemark describes the best transparent words and how to use them effectively.

List of grammar rules

Learning grammar is outside the scope of this book, however we will present one helpful approach here. A complete or nearly complete list of grammar rules can be prepared for each foreign language. Such a list will help you gauge the overall volume of information that must be learned. It will also help you understand which rules should be learned at the beginning stage and which can be learned later.

Schedule

In order to prevent your language study from turning into an uncontrolled process, you must establish landmarks and create some sort of schedule. You can plan a specific number of words to learn in a month, two months, or half of a year. You can set a goal to watch a certain number of movies and compose a list of books to read within a fixed period of time.

8.2 MEMORIZING WORDS

Mnemonics

Mnemonics is the science of remembering. It includes all approaches, methods, and tricks that facilitate remembering information. In this section we will present just a few examples. They have been taken from the personal experience of people who have actively studied languages for a long time. The ability to memorize is nothing other than possessing certain mnemonic skills.

Blocks of words

When you enter new words into your unified database, try to group them into small blocks of 3-5 words. This layout somewhat facilitates memorization, because even visually your records will look more organized. You may observe an additional association between the blocks of words, allowing you to combine them into a single chain, especially if the words are taken from the same source, e.g. the same book.

Paronyms

Paronyms are words having the same stem. This might be a noun, adjective, and verb with the same root (for example, in English: agreement, agreeable, to agree). If you come across paronyms while looking up the meaning of a new concept in the dictionary, include them in your unified database. This will let you easily learn an entire block of words associated with the same root.

Phrases

In many cases, a word can be more easily memorized by adding other words to it to create a phrase. For example, you can add an adjective to a noun, or an adverb to a verb (beautiful palace, to work hard). The more original the combination of words, the more memorable it will be. You can even try to create interesting bilingual phrases by adding a word from your native language rather than the foreign language.

Similar words

Easily remembered phrases can also be created by adding homophones or words will a similar form. These are words that are similar in pronunciation (whole-hole) or spelling (bear-beer). By combining these words with your original word, you can get a good mnemonic that will facilitate reliable memorization.

Atkinson method

This method was developed by the famous scientist and psychologist Richard Chatham Atkinson. The gist of the method is to pick a key word in your native language for a foreign word, and create a mental image that links the two concepts. The key word is chosen based on similarity of pronunciation with a foreign word. For example, PATO (Spanish: duck) and POT (English: pan). By forming a mental image or drawing a picture in which "duck" and "pot" are connected in an unusual manner, you end up with an association that is easy to remember.

Opposites

White-black, good-bad, heaven-hell – pairs of antonyms like these are one way to use mnemonics in a fun approach to remembering words. You can find similar word associations in the dictionary. Collections of such words are often encountered in topical dictionaries and phrasebooks.

Synonyms

Learning synonyms is generally not recommended at the beginning stages of study, because it increases the load on the brain and can introduce some confusion. But in many instances it is helpful to match a synonym with a source word, if you are having difficulty with it. The two synonyms may produce a novel, memorable combination. Using the Internet or specialized dictionaries is convenient for selecting these words.

Word in context

This is another mnemonic technique that promotes memorization of words. It is especially productive if you have a concordancer with a large corpus of the language being studied. You can also use any Internet search engine for this purpose. The goal is to find several sentences containing the word you are looking for. The words on the left and the right of your word, as well as the entire sentence, might suggest an associative chain that will result in memorization.

Memorizing in a list

You can use this method if you are keeping a notebook for new words or a unified word database. When you have accumulated a column of 20-30 new words, you simply review them at a moderate, comfortable pace without stopping long on each individual record. After 20-30 minutes try to translate this list from the foreign language into your native language, without peeking at the translation. You will discover that for some reason your brain has already remembered some of the words on its own. An occasional review will firmly fix what you have learned in your long-term memory.

Listening to blocks of words

If you have the ability to make an audio recording of new words (on your own or using text-to-speech technology), you will significantly diversify your work to review words. New material should be reviewed as often as possible. Therefore, after reviewing each new block of 5-10 words, we recommend reviewing and listening to the previous blocks. This can be done very quickly and isn't exhausting at all.

Change of medium

If you keep your working list of words in electronic form, sometimes it can help to transfer the file to a different device. For example, suppose you work primarily on a tablet computer. You can copy your file to an e-reader or phone, or print it on paper. Any change will stimulate your brain to work more actively.

Paper flash cards

These are a somewhat obsolete tool for working with vocabulary words. Nevertheless, it can still prove useful even today. The difference is that you shouldn't use them for every word, as has been done in the past, but only for those that are difficult to memorize. Flash cards are easy to make from heavy paper or cardboard. For languages where nouns have a gender, you can use colored paper. For example, make yellow flash cards for masculine nouns and blue flash cards for feminine nouns.

Flash-card smartphone apps

The developers of these apps position them as a tool for memorizing words, however they are more suitable for review. If you have an app that lets you enter your own words, you can use it to create a list of words you are unsure of. Periodically reviewing the flash cards will help you reliably memorize many of them.

Sticky notes

These are a type of homemade flash card for working with new words. The goal is to increase the number of visual encounters with each concept you need to remember. This is essentially a somewhat modified method of review. You write a difficult word on a sticky piece of paper and apply it to your house – on your mirror, refrigerator, door, or other place where you will be sure to see it.

Pictures

Another way to increase the probability of remembering a word is to match it with a picture. This can simply be a printout from the Internet that you will only need temporarily while you memorize the word. Advanced computer users can select images for almost all of the words in there unified word database and embed them directly in the file. For example, you can do this in Excel.

Create visual idiosyncrasies for words

In order to make a word more memorable, you can try to artistically create visual idiosyncrasies for it. For example, you can write the word on a flash card in a unique, unusual font, somehow highlight part of the word, capitalize one or more letters, etc. You can add some sort of pattern, symbol, or design to the way you write the word. Everything that makes a word stand apart from others will help you remember it better.

Review previous words

If you've made it your rule to learn words in small blocks, then after learning a new group of words, review one or two of the previous groups. This uncomplicated approach reinforces what you have learned and reveals the concepts that haven't yet taken root in your memory. You need to spend extra time on these words.

Progressively longer phrases

This is a great approach to simultaneously practice your pronunciation and memorize rather long sentences. Essentially, the approach is for you to split the desired phrase into small blocks of 2-3 words and say the sentence aloud in parts, gradually adding the next block to the first. Reviewing each sentence multiple times using this technique yields great results.

8.3 READING SKILLS

Read as much as possible

Reading is one the basic requirements for somebody using a foreign language. If the writing system of the language you are studying is the same as your native language, learning to read will be much easier than learning to speak or write. Reading develops lots of skills, promotes the memorization and reinforcement of words, and stimulates your visual memory. The more you read, the more substantial your progress will be and the faster you'll reach your goals.

Reading children's books

Because vocabulary is always so limited at the beginning stage, children's books can be a great developmental exercise. Books designed for children for children 6-12 years of age are especially beneficial. These publications contain simple words, rather easy phrases, as well as pictures that help you remember the words and phrases you encounter. Moreover, you will better understand the culture of the country you are interested in if you read books that the residents there typically read as children. This literature will become part of the country-specific information that will come in handy in the future.

Reading adapted books

Several properties make adapted books are extremely useful: They are generally short publications that you can realistically read through to the end; The works most frequently adapted are interesting to read at any age; Sometimes these books contain lists of the difficult words and clichés found in the text. Reading adapted books is an excellent preparatory step toward being able to switch to the original foreign works.

Reading on a specific topic

Reading online articles on a specific topic is an effective exercise, particularly at the beginning stages. You choose articles on a subject that you understand or find interesting. Then you read them with the help of a dictionary. In these texts you will encounter a large number of repeated, frequently-used words which should be added to your unified word database. After a while you will begin to understand well the basic content of similar articles, even without possessing a large vocabulary.

Audiobooks (printed book + CD)

You can only derive the maximum benefit from audiobooks in a foreign language if the audio recording includes the text in either printed or electronic form. You should listen to individual chapters after you have read them and written down the new words for translation. Audiobooks are an excellent tool to review new words from books and to strengthen your ability to comprehend foreign speech.

Reading subtitles to movies and shows

On the Internet you can find quite a large number of text subtitles to movies and shows. This is also fantastic material for reading, especially at the intermediate and advanced stages of learning. Subtitles resemble a book consisting of dialogs, e.g. conversational language. You can read them just like any other book, writing down new words and interesting phrases. If you have the subtitles in addition to the film, they become full-fledged study material.

8.4 REPETITION

System for reviewing words

When it comes to reinforcing new words in your long-term memory, what matters most is the number of repetitions and the quality of the association you have created for each word. This is easy enough with a few words, but when you have amassed more than a thousand you will need some kind of system to periodically review all the contents of your database.

Table method

If you have kept your new vocabulary words properly – as a table with columns for source words and the translations – then you can review them effectively. Print the desired subset; your working materials will be A4 paper. By hiding one column or the other, you can create test translations from the foreign language to your native language, or vice versa.

Review using audio

As an option, you can review words using an audio recording you've made yourself or with text-to-speech technology. Listening to audio recordings is less exhausting than reviewing words on a printout. In 20 minutes you can review approximately one thousand words. And you can do these exercises every day, which is extremely beneficial for reliably fixing words in your long-term memory.

Repetitive viewing of movies or shows

Foreign movies and shows in the original language are wonderful materials that should be used for learning purposes, especially if the film is accompanied by subtitles in the language you need. For educational viewing, select movies and shows that you can watch multiple times and which contain a large number of dialogs. You'll get the greatest benefit from this resource if you carefully work through all of the subtitles – read, write down new words, and find them in the dictionary.

Listening to songs

If you actively use songs and song lyrics in your study program, the repetitive listening will be an important part of your review of words. The proper way to use songs might be as follows: Read and translate the lyrics, write down new words into your word database, and do the work to learn them. Then listening to your favorites songs will become both enjoyable and beneficial.

Re-reading books

Re-reading a book or a collection of related articles can be a great way to re-inforce words and test how well you remember them. In order for this process to be truly productive, you must approach it properly from the very start: select a book that you would to read again. Each time you re-read a book, your con-fidence in your abilities is strengthened.

Review using audiobooks

It's best if you've ensured that you have comprehensive study materials and that your reading books are supplemented with audiobooks. Once you have read a book through, and written down and learned the new words, you should review all the material. An audiobook lets you listen to the text of a book as many times as you'd like, without any great effort.

Audio dictionary

An audio dictionary is a list of words that exist simultaneously in printed form and on an audio device. You can try to buy a ready-made dictionary or create your own. In either case, all the words in the dictionary should be added to your unified word database. The main purpose of such an aid is to review new words after you've actively worked to memorize them.

Flash-card smartphone apps

At present, a large number of mobile apps have been developed for improving your foreign language skills. Apps like memocards are good tools for review-ing words. The most interesting programs are those that let you build your own list of words by copying information from your unified word database.

8.5 SUPPLEMENTARY TECHNOLOGIES

Internet

The worldwide web is an inexhaustible source of useful materials: text, graphics, photos, audio, and video. The Internet lets you find material in any language in the world. Additionally, it provides a huge body of interesting country-specific information. You'll find language courses and reference books on grammar, phonetics, and other aspects of the foreign language you are interested in. The Internet is increasingly replacing television, over-the-air radio, and traditional newspapers and textbooks.

Text-to-speech

Text-to-speech (TTS, speech synthesis) is a digital technology that can reproduce any text in a human voice. TTS is typically provided by a computer program; a voice in the language you need is loaded into the program. All of these programs are far from perfect, but you can try to use them for educational purposes to listen to texts, word lists, and individual phrases and combinations of words. You can use TTS to record new words and listen to them aloud repeatedly.

Contextual translators

Some electronic dictionaries have a feature that lets you instantaneously receive a translation of an incomprehensible text. You simply move the cursor to the desired word and a window pops up with the translation. This is generally applicable to all types of computers, including tablet devices. These dictionaries can be very expensive, but they save significant amounts of time when reading a book in the original and other difficult foreign texts.

Google Translate

Google, well-known for its search engine, offers a multitude of different services, including a machine translation service called Google Translate. This tool supports more than 50 language pairs. Google's translation algorithm, which is described as statistical machine translation, is adequate, but it still cannot be used with complete confidence. Google Translate can be used to get a general idea of the content of an article, web page, etc.

Topical dictionaries

Topical dictionaries of generally-used words can become an excellent source for adding to your vocabulary, especially at the beginning stage. These books are usually conveniently organized and contain the most important words of a foreign language. Topical dictionaries should be used as a supplement to the textbooks and audio materials you've included in your main study program.

JAPANESE VOCABULARY

This dictionary contains 1,500 frequently used words that will help you develop basic vocabulary. The dictionary's content is organized by topic. The material is presented in three columns: source word, translation, and transcription. Each topic consists of 50 words grouped into small blocks. You can treat this dictionary as a model for creating your own unified word database.

TIME. CALENDAR

time	時間	jikan
hour	時間	jikan
half an hour	半時間	han jikan
minute	分	bun
second	秒	byō

today (adv)	今日	kyō
tomorrow (adv)	明日	ashita
yesterday (adv)	昨日	kinō

Monday	月曜日	getsuyōbi
Tuesday	火曜日	kayōbi
Wednesday	水曜日	suiyōbi
Thursday	木曜日	mokuyōbi
Friday	金曜日	kinyōbi
Saturday	土曜日	doyōbi
Sunday	日曜日	nichiyōbi

day	日	nichi
workday	仕事日	shigoto bi
public holiday	祝日	shukujitsu
weekend	週末	shūmatsu

week	週	shū
last week (adv)	先週	senshū
next week (adv)	来週	raishū

sunrise	日の出	hinode
sunset	夕日	yūhi

in the morning	朝に	asa ni
in the afternoon	午後に	gogo ni

in the evening	夕方に	yūgata ni
tonight (this evening)	今晩	konban

at night	夜に	yoru ni
midnight	半夜	hanya

January	一月	ichigatsu
February	二月	nigatsu

March	三月	sangatsu
April	四月	shigatsu
May	五月	gogatsu
June	六月	rokugatsu

July	七月	shichigatsu
August	八月	hachigatsu
September	九月	kugatsu
October	十月	jūgatsu
November	十一月	jūichigatsu
December	十二月	jūnigatsu

in spring	春に	haru ni
in summer	夏に	natsu ni
in fall	秋に	aki ni
in winter	冬に	fuyu ni

month	月	tsuki
season (summer, etc.)	季節	kisetsu
year	年	toshi
century	世紀	seiki

NUMBERS. NUMERALS

digit, figure	数字、 桁数	sūji, keta sū
number	数字	sūji
minus	マイナス	mainasu
plus	加号、 プラス	ka gō, purasu
sum, total	合計	gōkei
first (adj)	第一の	dai ichi no
second (adj)	第二の	dai ni no
third (adj)	第三の	dai san no
0 zero	ゼロ	zero
1 one	一	ichi
2 two	二	ni
3 three	三	san
4 four	四	yon
5 five	五	go
6 six	六	roku
7 seven	七	nana
8 eight	八	hachi
9 nine	九	kyū
10 ten	十	jū
11 eleven	十一	jū ichi
12 twelve	十二	jū ni
13 thirteen	十三	jū san
14 fourteen	十四	jū yon
15 fifteen	十五	jū go
16 sixteen	十六	jū roku
17 seventeen	十七	jū nana
18 eighteen	十八	jū hachi
19 nineteen	十九	jū kyū
20 twenty	二十	ni jū
30 thirty	三十	san jū
40 forty	四	yon
50 fifty	五十	go jū
60 sixty	六十	roku jū
70 seventy	七十	nana jū
80 eighty	八十	yaso
90 ninety	九十	kyū jū

100 one hundred	百	hyaku
200 two hundred	二百	ni hyaku
300 three hundred	三百	san hyaku
400 four hundred	四百	yon hyaku
500 five hundred	五百	go hyaku
600 six hundred	六百	roku hyaku
700 seven hundred	七百	nana hyaku
800 eight hundred	八百	hachi hyaku
900 nine hundred	九百	kyū hyaku
1000 one thousand	千	sen
10000 ten thousand	一万	ichi man
one hundred thousand	10万	jū man
million	百万	hyaku man
billion	十億	jū oku

HUMANS. FAMILY

man (adult male)	男性	dansei
young man	若者	wakamono
teenager	ティーンエージャー	tīnējā
woman	女性	josei
girl (young woman)	少女	shōjo
age	年齢	nenrei
adult	大人	otona
middle-aged (adj)	中年の	chūnen no
elderly (adj)	年配の	nenpai no
old (adj)	古い	furui
old man	老人	rōjin
old woman	老婦人	rō fujin
retirement	退職	taishoku
to retire (from job)	退職する	taishoku suru
retiree	退職者	taishoku sha
mother	母親	hahaoya
father	父親	chichioya
son	息子	musuko
daughter	娘	musume
brother	弟	otōto
sister	妹	imōto
parents	親	oya
child	子供	kodomo
children	子供	kodomo
stepmother	継母	keibo
stepfather	継父	keifu
grandmother	祖母	sobo
grandfather	祖父	sofu
grandson	男の孫	otoko no mago
granddaughter	孫娘	magomusume
grandchildren	孫	mago
uncle	伯父	oji
aunt	伯母	oba
nephew	甥	oi
niece	姪	mei

wife	妻	tsuma
husband	夫	otto
married (masc.)	既婚の	kikon no
married (fem.)	既婚の	kikon no
widow	未亡人	mibōjin
widower	男やもめ	otokoyamome
name, first name	名前	namae
family name	姓	sei
relative	親戚	shinseki
friend (masc.)	友人	yūjin
friendship	友情	yūjō
partner	相手	aite
superior	上司	jōshi
colleague	同僚	dōryō
neighbors	隣人	rinjin

HUMAN BODY

organism	人体	jintai
body	身体	shintai
heart	心臓	shinzō
blood	血液	ketsueki
brain	脳	nō
nerve	神経	shinkei

bone	骨	hone
skeleton	骸骨	gaikotsu
spine	背骨	sebone
rib	肋骨	rokkotsu
skull	頭蓋骨	zugaikotsu

muscle	筋肉	kinniku
lungs	肺臓	haizō
skin	肌	hada

head	頭	atama
face	顔	kao
nose	鼻	hana
forehead	額	gaku
cheek	頬	hō

mouth	口	kuchi
tongue	舌	shita
tooth	歯	ha
lips	唇	kuchibiru
chin	あご	ago

ear	耳	mimi
neck	首	kubi
throat	喉	nodo

eye	眼	me
pupil	瞳	hitomi
eyebrow	眉	mayu
eyelash	睫毛	matsuge

hair	髪の毛	kaminoke
hairstyle	髪型	kamigata
mustache	口ひげ	kuchihige

beard	あごひげ	agohige
to have (a beard, etc.)	…がある	... ga aru
bald (adj)	禿げた	hage ta
hand	手	te
arm	腕	ude
finger	指	yubi
nail	爪	tsume
palm	手のひら	tenohira
shoulder	肩	kata
leg	足、　脚	ashi, ashi
foot	足	ashi
knee	膝	hiza
heel	踵	kakato
back	背中	senaka
waist	腰	koshi
beauty mark	ほくろ	hokuro
birthmark	あざ	aza

MEDICINE. DISEASES. DRUGS.

health	健康	kenkō
healthy (adj)	健康な	kenkō na
sickness	病気	byōki
to be sick	病気になる	byōki ni naru
ill, sick (adj)	病気の	byōki no
cold (illness)	風邪	kaze
to catch a cold	風邪をひく	kaze o hiku
tonsillitis	扁桃腺炎	hentōsen en
pneumonia	肺炎	haien
flu, influenza	流感	ryūkan
runny nose (coryza)	鼻水	hanamizu
cough	咳	seki
to cough (vi)	咳をする	seki o suru
to sneeze (vi)	くしゃみをする	kushami o suru
stroke	脳卒中	nōsocchū
heart attack	心臓発作	shinzō hossa
allergy	アレルギー	arerugī
asthma	喘息	zensoku
diabetes	糖尿病	tōnyō byō
tumor	腫瘍	shuyō
cancer	癌	gan
alcoholism	アルコール依存症	arukōru izon shō
AIDS	エイズ	eizu
fever	発熱	hatsunetsu
seasickness	船酔い	fune yoi
bruise (hématome)	打ち身	uchimi
bump (lump)	たんこぶ	tankobu
to limp (vi)	足を引きずる	ashi o hikizuru
dislocation	脱臼	dakkyū
to dislocate (vt)	脱臼する	dakkyū suru
fracture	骨折	kossetsu
burn (injury)	火傷	kashō
injury	負傷	fushō
pain	痛み	itami
toothache	歯痛	shitsū

to sweat (perspire)	汗をかく	ase o kaku
deaf (adj)	難聴の	nanchō no
dumb (adj)	唖の	oshi no

immunity	免疫	meneki
virus	ウィルス	wirusu
microbe	細菌	saikin
bacterium	バクテリア	bakuteria
infection	伝染	densen

hospital	病院	byōin
cure	治療	chiryō
to vaccinate (vt)	予防接種をする	yobō sesshu o suru
to be in a coma	昏睡状態である	konsui jōtai de aru
intensive care	集中治療	shūchū chiryō
symptom	兆候	chōkō
pulse	脈拍	myakuhaku

FEELINGS. EMOTIONS. CONVERSATION

I, me	私	watashi
you	あなた	anata
he	彼	kare
she	彼女	kanojo
we	私たち	watashi tachi
you (to a group)	あなたがた	anata ga ta
they	彼らは	karera wa
Hello! (fam.)	ハロー! やあ!	harō, yā
Hello! (form.)	こんにちは!	konnichiwa
Good morning!	おはようございます!	ohayō gozai masu
Good afternoon!	こんにちは!	konnichiwa
Good evening!	こんばんは!	konbanwa
to say hello	挨拶をする	aisatsu o suru
to greet (vt)	挨拶する	aisatsu suru
How are you?	元気?	genki?
Bye-Bye! Goodbye!	さようなら!	sayōnara
Thank you!	ありがとう!	arigatō
feelings	感情	kanjō
to be hungry	空かす	sukasu
to be thirsty	渇く	kawaku
tired (adj)	疲れた	tsukare ta
to be worried	心配する	shinpai suru
to be nervous	神経を使う	shinkei o tsukau
hope	希望	kibō
to hope (vi, vt)	望む	nozomu
character	性格	seikaku
modest (adj)	謙遜な	kenson na
lazy (adj)	怠惰な	taida na
generous (adj)	気前のよい	kimae no yoi
talented (adj)	才能のある	sainō no aru
honest (adj)	正直な	shōjiki na
serious (adj)	真剣な	shinken na
shy, timid (adj)	内気な	uchiki na
sincere (adj)	誠実な	seijitsu na
coward	臆病者	okubyōmono

to sleep (vi)	眠る	nemuru
dream	夢	yume
bed	ベッド	beddo
pillow	枕	makura

insomnia	不眠症	fuminshō
to go to bed	就寝する	shūshin suru
nightmare	悪夢	akumu
alarm clock	目覚まし時計	mezamashi tokei

smile	微笑み	hohoemi
to smile (vi)	微笑む	hohoemu
to laugh (vi)	笑う	warau

quarrel	口論	kōron
insult	侮辱、 無礼	bujoku, burei
offense (to take ~)	立腹	rippuku
angry (mad)	怒る	okoru

CLOTHING. PERSONAL ACCESSORIES

clothes	衣服	ifuku
overcoat	コート	kōto
fur coat	毛皮のコート	kegawa no kōto
jacket (e.g., leather ~)	ジャンパー	janpā
raincoat	レインコート	reinkōto
shirt	ワイシャツ	waishatsu
pants	ズボン	zubon
jacket (of man's suit)	ジャケット	jaketto
suit	背広	sebiro
dress (frock)	ドレス	doresu
skirt	スカート	sukāto
T-shirt	Tシャツ	tei shatsu
bathrobe	バスローブ	basurōbu
pajamas	パジャマ	pajama
workwear	仕事着	shigoto gi
underwear	下着	shitagi
socks	靴下	kutsushita
bra	ブラジャー	burajā
pantyhose	タイツ	taitsu
stockings	ストッキング	sutokkingu
bathing suit	水着	mizugi
hat	帽子	bōshi
footwear	履物	hakimono
boots (cowboy ~)	ブーツ	būtsu
heel	踵	kakato
shoestring	靴ひも	kutsu himo
shoe polish	靴墨	kutsuzumi
cotton (n)	綿	men
wool (n)	羊毛	yōmō
fur (n)	毛皮	kegawa
gloves	手袋	tebukuro
mittens	ミトン	miton
scarf (long)	マフラー	mafurā
glasses	眼鏡	megane
umbrella	雨傘	amagasa

necktie	ネクタイ	nekutai
handkerchief	ハンカチ	hankachi
comb	櫛、くし	kushi, kushi
hairbrush	ヘアブラシ	hea burashi

buckle	バックル	bakkuru
belt	ベルト	beruto
purse	ハンドバッグ	handobaggu

collar	襟	eri
pocket	ポケット	poketto
sleeve	袖	sode
fly (on trousers)	ズボンのファスナー	zubon no fasunā

zipper (fastener)	チャック	chakku
button	ボタン	botan
to get dirty (vi)	汚れる	yogoreru
stain (mark, spot)	染み	shimi

CITY. URBAN INSTITUTIONS

store	店、 屋	mise, ya
shopping mall	ショッピングモール	shoppingu mōru
supermarket	スーパーマーケット	sūpāmāketto
shoe store	靴屋	kutsu ya
bookstore	本屋	honya
drugstore, pharmacy	ドラッグストア	doraggusutoa
bakery	パン屋	pan ya
cake store	菓子店	kashi ten
grocery store	食料品店	shokuryō hin ten
butcher shop	肉屋	nikuya
produce store	八百屋	yaoya
market	市場	shijō
hair salon	理髪室	rihatsu shitsu
post office	郵便局	yūbin kyoku
dry cleaners	ドライクリーニング店	doraikurīningu ten
circus	サーカス	sākasu
zoo	動物園	dōbutsu en
theater	劇場	gekijō
movie theater	映画館	eiga kan
museum	博物館	hakubutsukan
library	図書館	toshokan
mosque	モスク	mosuku
synagogue	シナゴーグ	shinagōgu
cathedral	大聖堂	dai seidō
temple	寺院	jiin
church	教会	kyōkai
institute	大学	daigaku
university	大学	daigaku
school	学校	gakkō
hotel	ホテル	hoteru
bank	銀行	ginkō
embassy	大使館	taishikan
travel agency	旅行代理店	ryokō dairi ten
subway	地下鉄	chikatetsu
hospital	病院	byōin

gas station	ガソリンスタンド	gasorinsutando
parking lot	駐車場	chūsha jō

ENTRANCE	入口	iriguchi
EXIT	出口	ideguchi
PUSH	押す	osu
PULL	引く	hiku
OPEN	営業中	eigyō chū
CLOSED	休業	kyūgyō

monument	記念碑	kinen hi
fortress	要塞	yōsai
palace	宮殿	kyūden

medieval (adj)	中世の	chūsei no
ancient (adj)	古代の	kodai no
national (adj)	国の	kuni no
well-known (adj)	有名な	yūmei na

MONEY. FINANCES

money	金銭	kinsen
coin	コイン	koin
dollar	ドル	doru
euro	ユーロ	yūro
ATM	キャッシュマシーン	kyasshumashīn
money exchange	両替所	ryōgae sho
exchange rate	両替レート	ryōgae rēto
cash	現金	genkin
How much?	いくら?	ikura?
to pay (vi, vt)	払う	harau
payment	支払い	shiharai
change (give the ~)	おつり	o tsuri
price	価格	kakaku
discount	割引	waribiki
cheap (adj)	安い	yasui
expensive (adj)	高い	takai
bank	銀行	ginkō
account	口座	kōza
credit card	クレジットカード	kurejittokādo
check	小切手	kogitte
to write a check	小切手を切る	kogitte o kiru
checkbook	小切手帳	kogitte chō
debt	借金	shakkin
debtor	債務者	saimu sha
to lend (money)	貸す	kasu
to borrow (vi, vt)	借りる	kariru
to rent (~ a tuxedo)	借りる	kariru
on credit (adv)	クレジットカードで	kurejittokādo de
wallet	札入れ	satsuire
safe	金庫	kinko
inheritance	相続	sōzoku
fortune (wealth)	富	tomi
tax	税	zei
fine	罰金	bakkin

to fine (vt)	罰金を科す	bakkin o kasu
wholesale (adj)	卸売りの	oroshiuri no
retail (adj)	小売の	kouri no
to insure (vt)	保険をつける	hoken o tsukeru
insurance	保険	hoken
capital	資本	shihon
turnover	生産高	seisan daka
stock (share)	株	kabu
profit	利益	rieki
profitable (adj)	利益のある	rieki no aru
crisis	危機	kiki
bankruptcy	破産	hasan
to go bankrupt	破産する	hasan suru
accountant	会計係	kaikei gakari
salary	給料	kyūryō
bonus (money)	ボーナス	bōnasu

TRANSPORTATION

bus	バス	basu
streetcar	路面電車	romen densha
trolley	トロリーバス	tororībasu
to go by ...	...で行く	... de iku
to get on (~ the bus)	乗る	noru
to get off ...	降りる	oriru
stop (e.g., bus ~)	停	toma
terminus	終点	shūten
schedule	時刻表	jikoku hyō
ticket	切符	kippu
to be late (for ...)	遅れる	okureru
taxi, cab	タクシー	takushī
by taxi	タクシーで	takushī de
taxi stand	タクシー乗り場	takushī noriba
traffic	交通	kōtsū
rush hour	ラッシュアワー	rasshuawā
to park (vi)	駐車する	chūsha suru
subway	地下鉄	chikatetsu
station	駅	eki
train	列車	ressha
train station	駅	eki
rails	レール	rēru
compartment	コンパートメント	konpātomento
berth	寝台	shindai
airplane	航空機	kōkūki
air ticket	航空券	kōkū ken
airline	航空会社	kōkū kaisha
airport	空港	kūkō
flight (act of flying)	飛行	hikō
luggage	荷物	nimotsu
luggage cart	荷物カート	nimotsu kāto
ship	船	fune
ocean liner	クルーズ客船	kurūzu kyakusen
yacht	クルーザー	kurūzā

boat (flat-bottomed ~)	ボート	bōto
captain	船長	senchō
cabin	船室	senshitsu
port (harbor)	港	minato

bicycle	自転車	jitensha
scooter	スクーター	sukūtā
motorcycle, bike	オートバイ	ōtobai
pedal	ペダル	pedaru
pump	ポンプ	ponpu
wheel	車輪	sharin

automobile, car	自動車	jidōsha
ambulance	救急車	kyūkyū sha
truck	トラック	torakku
second hand (adj)	中古	chūko
car accident	車の事故	kuruma no jiko
repair	修理	shūri

FOOD. PART 1

meat	肉	niku
chicken	鶏肉	keiniku
duck	アヒル	ahiru

pork	豚肉	butaniku
veal	子牛の肉	ko ushi no niku
lamb	子羊の肉	kohitsuji no niku
beef	牛肉	gyūniku

sausage (salami, etc.)	ソーセージ	sōsēji
egg	卵	tamago
fish	魚	sakana
cheese	チーズ	chīzu
sugar	砂糖	satō
salt	塩	shio

rice	米	bei
pasta	マカロニ	makaroni
butter	バター	batā
vegetable oil	植物油	shokubutsu yu
bread	パン	pan
chocolate (n)	チョコレート	chokorēto

wine	ワイン	wain
coffee	コーヒー	kōhī
milk	ミルク	miruku
juice	ジュース	jūsu
beer	ビール	bīru
tea	茶	cha

tomato	トマト	tomato
cucumber	胡瓜	kyūri
carrot	ニンジン	ninjin
potato	ジャガイモ	jagaimo
onion	玉葱	tamanegi

garlic	ニンニク	ninniku
cabbage	キャベツ	kyabetsu
beetroot	ビート	bīto
eggplant	ナス	nasu
dill	ディル	diru

| lettuce | レタス | retasu |
| corn (maize) | トウモロコシ | tōmorokoshi |

fruit	果物	kudamono
apple	りんご	ringo
pear	洋梨	yōnashi
lemon	レモン	remon
orange	オレンジ	orenji
strawberry	イチゴ	ichigo

plum	プラム	puramu
raspberry	木苺	kiichigo
pineapple	パイナップル	painappuru
banana	バナナ	banana
watermelon	西瓜	suika
grape	葡萄	budō
melon	メロン	meron

FOOD. PART 2

cuisine	料理	ryōri
recipe	レシピ	reshipi
food	食べ物	tabemono
to have breakfast	朝食をとる	chōshoku o toru
to have lunch	昼食をとる	chūshoku o toru
to have dinner	夕食をとる	yūshoku o toru
taste, flavor	味	aji
tasty (adj)	美味しい	oishii
cold (adj)	寒い、冷たい	samui, tsumetai
hot (adj)	熱い	atsui
sweet (sugary)	甘い	amai
salty (adj)	塩味の	shioaji no
sandwich (bread)	サンドイッチ	sandoicchi
garnish	付け合わせ	tsukeawase
filling (for cake, pie)	フィリング	firingu
sauce	ソース	sōsu
piece (of cake, pie)	一片	ippen
diet	ダイエット	daietto
vitamin	ビタミン	bitamin
calorie	カロリー	karorī
vegetarian (n)	菜食主義者	saishoku shugi sha
restaurant	レストラン	resutoran
coffee house	喫茶店	kissaten
appetite	食欲	shokuyoku
Enjoy your meal!	どうぞお召し上がり下さい!	dōzo o meshiagarikudasai
waiter	ウェイター	weitā
waitress	ウェートレス	wētoresu
bartender	バーテンダー	bātendā
menu	メニュー	menyū
spoon	スプーン	supūn
knife	ナイフ	naifu
fork	フォーク	fōku
cup (of coffee)	カップ	kappu

plate (dinner ~)	皿	sara
saucer	小皿	kozara
napkin (on table)	ナフキン	nafukin
toothpick	爪楊枝	tsumayōji
to order (meal)	注文する	chūmon suru
course, dish	料理	ryōri
portion	人前	hitomae
appetizer	前菜	zensai
salad	サラダ	sarada
soup	スープ	sūpu
dessert	デザート	dezāto
whole fruit jam	ジャム	jamu
ice-cream	アイスクリーム	aisukurīmu
check	お勘定	o kanjō
to pay the check	勘定を払う	kanjō o harau
tip	チップ	chippu

HOUSE. APARTMENT. PART 1

house	家屋	kaoku
country house	カントリーハウス	kantorī hausu
villa (by sea)	別荘	bessō
floor, story	階	kai
entrance	玄関	genkan
wall	壁	kabe
roof	屋根	yane
chimney (stack)	煙突	entotsu
loft (attic)	屋根裏	yaneura
window	窓	mado
window ledge	窓台	mado dai
balcony	バルコニー	barukonī
stairs (stairway)	階段	kaidan
mailbox	郵便箱	yūbinbako
trash container	ゴミ箱	gomibako
elevator	エレベーター	erebētā
electricity	電気	denki
light bulb	電球	denkyū
switch	スイッチ	suicchi
wall socket	コンセント	konsento
fuse	ヒューズ	hyūzu
door	ドア	doa
handle, doorknob	ドアノブ	doa nobu
key	鍵	kagi
doormat	ドアマット	doa matto
door lock	錠	jō
doorbell	ドアベル	doa beru
knock (at the door)	ノック	nokku
to knock (vi)	ノックする	nokku suru
peephole	ドアアイ	doaai
courtyard	中庭	nakaniwa
garden	庭	niwa
swimming pool	プール	pūru
gym	トレーニングジム	torēningujimu

tennis court	テニスコート	tenisu kōto
garage	ガレージ	garēji
private property	私有財産	shiyū zaisan
warning sign	警告表示	keikoku hyōji
security	警備	keibi
security guard	警備員	keibi in

renovations	リフォーム	rifōmu
to renovate (vt)	リフォームする	rifōmu suru
to put in order	片付ける	katazukeru
to paint (~ a wall)	塗る	nuru
wallpaper	壁紙	kabegami
to varnish (vt)	ニスを塗る	nisu o nuru

pipe	管	kan
tools	工具	kōgu
basement	地下室	chika shitsu
sewerage (system)	下水道	gesuidō

HOUSE. APARTMENT. PART 2

apartment	アパート	apāto
room	部屋	heya
bedroom	寝室	shinshitsu
dining room	ダイニングルーム	dainingu rūmu
living room	客間	kyakuma
study	書斎	shosai
entry room	玄関	genkan
bathroom	浴室	yokushitsu
half bath	トイレ	toire
floor	床	yuka
ceiling	天井	tenjō
to dust (vt)	ほこりを払う	hokori o harau
vacuum cleaner	掃除機	sōji ki
to vacuum (vt)	掃除機をかける	sōji ki o kakeru
mop	モップ	moppu
dust cloth	雑巾	zōkin
broom	重宝箒	chōhō hōki
dustpan	ちりとり	chiritori
furniture	家具	kagu
table	テーブル	tēburu
chair	椅子	isu
armchair	安楽椅子	anrakuisu
bookcase	本棚	hondana
shelf	棚	tana
wardrobe	洋服ダンス	yōfuku dansu
mirror	鏡	kagami
carpet	カーペット	kāpetto
fireplace	暖炉	danro
drapes	カーテン	kāten
table lamp	デスクスタンド	desuku sutando
chandelier	シャンデリア	shanderia
kitchen	台所	daidokoro
gas stove	ガスレンジ	gasurenji

electric stove	電気こんろ	denki kon ro
microwave oven	電子レンジ	denshi renji
refrigerator	冷蔵庫	reizōko
freezer	冷凍庫	reitōko
dishwasher	食器洗い機	shokkiarai ki
tap, faucet	蛇口	jaguchi
meat grinder	肉挽き器	niku hiki ki
juicer	ジューサー	jūsā
toaster	トースター	tōsutā
mixer	ミキサー	mikisā
coffee maker	コーヒーメーカー	kōhī mēkā
kettle	やかん	yakan
teapot	急須	kyūsu
TV set	テレビ	terebi
video, VCR	ビデオテープレコーダー	bideo tēpurekōdā
iron (e.g., steam ~)	アイロン	airon
telephone	電話	denwa

PROFESSIONS. SOCIAL STATUS

director	責任者	sekinin sha
superior	上司	jōshi
president	会頭	kaitō
assistant	助手	joshu
secretary	秘書	hisho
owner, proprietor	経営者	keiei sha
partner	相手	aite
stockholder	株主	kabunushi
businessman	ビジネスマン	bijinesuman
millionaire	百万長者	hyakumanchōja
billionaire	億万長者	oku man chōja
actor	俳優	haiyū
architect	建築士	kenchiku shi
banker	銀行家	ginkō ka
broker	ブローカー	burōkā
veterinarian	獣医	jūi
doctor	医者	isha
chambermaid	客室係	kyakushitsu gakari
designer	デザイナー	dezainā
correspondent	記者	kisha
delivery man	宅配業者	takuhai gyōsha
electrician	電気工	denki kō
musician	音楽家	ongakuka
babysitter	ベビーシッター	bebīshittā
hairdresser	理髪師	rihatsu shi
herdsman	牧夫	bokufu
singer (masc.)	歌手	kashu
translator	翻訳者	honyaku sha
writer	作家	sakka
carpenter	大工	daiku
cook	料理人	ryōri jin
fireman	消防士	shōbō shi
policeman	警官	keikan
mailman	郵便配達人	yūbin haitatsu jin
programmer	プログラマー	puroguramā

salesman	店員	tenin
worker	労働者	rōdō sha
gardener	庭師	niwashi
plumber	配管工	haikan kō
stomatologist	歯科医	shika i
flight attendant	客室乗務員	kyakushitsu jōmu in
dancer (masc.)	ダンサー	dansā
bodyguard	ボディーガード	bodīgādo
scientist	科学者	kagaku sha
teacher	教師	kyōshi
(in primary school)		
farmer	ファーマー	fāmā
surgeon	外科医	geka i
miner	鉱山労働者	kōzan rōdō sha
chef	料理人	ryōri jin
driver	運転手	unten shu

SPORT

kind of sports	競技種目	kyōgi shumoku
soccer	サッカー	sakkā
hockey	アイスホッケー	aisuhokkē
basketball	バスケットボール	basukettobōru
baseball	野球	yakyū
volleyball	バレーボール	barēbōru
boxing	ボクシング	bokushingu
wrestling	レスリング	resuringu
tennis	テニス	tenisu
swimming	水泳	suiei
chess	チェス	chesu
running	ランニング	ranningu
athletics	陸上競技	rikujō kyōgi
figure skating	フィギュアスケート	figyua sukēto
cycling	サイクリング	saikuringu
billiards	ビリヤード	biriyādo
bodybuilding	ボディビル	bodibiru
golf	ゴルフ	gorufu
diving	潜水	sensui
sailing	セーリング	sēringu
archery	洋弓	yōkyū
period, half	ピリオド、ハーフ	piriodo, hāfu
half-time	ハーフタイム	hāfutaimu
draw	引き分け	hikiwake
to draw (vi)	引き分けになる	hikiwake ni naru
treadmill	トレッドミル	toreddomiru
player	競技者	kyōgi sha
substitute	補欠選手	hoketsu senshu
substitutes bench	補欠選手ベンチ	hoketsu senshu benchi
match	試合	shiai
goal	サッカーゴール	sakkā gōru
goalkeeper	ゴールキーパー	gōrukīpā
goal (score)	ゴール	gōru
Olympic Games	オリンピック	orinpikku
to set a record	記録を打ち立てる	kiroku o uchitateru

final	決勝戦	kesshō sen
champion	チャンピオン	chanpion
championship	選手権	senshuken
winner	勝利者	shōri sha
victory	勝利	shōri
to win (vi)	勝つ	katsu
to lose (not win)	負ける	makeru
medal	メダル	medaru
first place	一位	ichi i
second place	二位	ni i
third place	三位	san i
stadium	スタジアム	sutajiamu
fan, supporter	ファン	fan
trainer, coach	トレーナー	torēnā
training	トレーニング	torēningu

FOREIGN LANGUAGES. ORTHOGRAPHY

language	言語	gengo
to study (vt)	学ぶ	manabu
pronunciation	発音	hatsuon
accent	なまり	namari
noun	名詞	meishi
adjective	形容詞	keiyōshi
verb	動詞	dōshi
adverb	副詞	fukushi
pronoun	代名詞	daimeishi
interjection	間投詞	kantōshi
preposition	前置詞	zenchishi
root	語根	gokon
ending	語尾	gobi
prefix	接頭辞	settō ji
syllable	音節	onsetsu
suffix	接尾辞	setsubi ji
stress mark	アクセント	akusento
period, dot	点	ten
comma	コンマ	konma
colon	コロン	koron
ellipsis	リーダー	rīdā
question	質問	shitsumon
question mark	疑問符	gimonfu
exclamation point	感嘆符	kantan fu
in quotation marks	二重引用符で囲む	ni jū inyō fu de kakomu
in parenthesis	カッコ内	kakko nai
letter	文字	moji
capital letter	大文字	daimonji
sentence	文	bun
word group	語結合	katari ketsugō
expression	表現	hyōgen
subject	主語	shugo
predicate	述語	jutsugo
line	ライン	rain

paragraph	段落	danraku
synonym	同義語	dōgi go
antonym	反意語	hanigo
exception	除外	jogai
to underline (vt)	下線を引く	kasen o hiku
rules	規則	kisoku
grammar	文法	bunpō
vocabulary	語彙	goi
phonetics	音声学	onsei gaku
alphabet	アルファベット	arufabetto
textbook	教科書	kyōkasho
dictionary	辞書	jisho
phrasebook	実用会話書	jitsuyō kaiwa sho
word	単語	tango
meaning	意味	imi
memory	記憶	kioku

THE EARTH. GEOGRAPHY

the Earth	地球	chikyū
globe (the Earth)	地球	chikyū
planet	惑星	wakusei

geography	地理学	chiri gaku
nature	自然	shizen
map	地図	chizu
atlas	地図帳	chizu chō

in the north	北に	kita ni
in the south	南に	minami ni
in the west	西に	nishi ni
in the east	東に	higashi ni

sea	海	umi
ocean	海洋	kaiyō
gulf (bay)	湾	wan
straits	海峡	kaikyō

continent (mainland)	大陸	tairiku
island	島	shima
peninsula	半島	hantō
archipelago	群島	guntō

harbor	港湾	kōwan
coral reef	サンゴ礁	sangoshō
shore	海岸	kaigan
coast	沿岸	engan

| high tide | 満潮 | manchō |
| low tide | 干潮 | kanchō |

latitude	緯度	ido
longitude	経度	keido
parallel	緯線	isen
equator	赤道	sekidō

sky	空	sora
horizon	地平	chihei
atmosphere	大気	taiki
mountain	山	yama

summit, top	頂上	chōjō
cliff	崖	gake
hill	丘	oka
volcano	火山	kazan
glacier	氷河	hyōga
waterfall	滝	taki
plain	平原	heigen
river	川	kawa
spring (natural source)	泉	izumi
bank (of river)	川岸	kawagishi
downstream (adv)	下流の	karyū no
upstream (adv)	上流の	jōryū no
lake	湖	mizuumi
dam	ダム	damu
canal	運河	unga
swamp, bog	沼地	numachi
ice	氷	kōri

COUNTRIES OF THE WORLD. PART 1

Europe	ヨーロッパ	yōroppa
European Union	欧州連合	ōshū rengō
European (n)	ヨーロッパ人	yōroppa jin
European (adj)	ヨーロッパの	yōroppa no
Austria	オーストリア	ōsutoria
Great Britain	大ブリテン島	dai buri ten tō
England	イギリス	igirisu
Belgium	ベルギー	berugī
Germany	ドイツ	doitsu
Netherlands	オランダ	oranda
Holland	オランダ	oranda
Greece	ギリシア	girishia
Denmark	デンマーク	denmāku
Ireland	アイルランド	airurando
Iceland	アイスランド	aisurando
Spain	スペイン	supein
Italy	イタリア	itaria
Cyprus	キプロス	kipurosu
Malta	マルタ	maruta
Norway	ノルウェー	noruwē
Portugal	ポルトガル	porutogaru
Finland	フィンランド	finrando
France	フランス	furansu
Sweden	スウェーデン	suwēden
Switzerland	スイス	suisu
Scotland	スコットランド	sukottorando
Vatican	バチカン	bachikan
Liechtenstein	リヒテンシュタイン	rihitenshutain
Luxembourg	ルクセンブルク	rukusenburuku
Monaco	モナコ	monako
Albania	アルバニア	arubania
Bulgaria	ブルガリア	burugaria
Hungary	ハンガリー	hangarī
Latvia	ラトビア	ratobia
Lithuania	リトアニア	ritoania

Poland	ポーランド	pōrando
Romania	ルーマニア	rūmania
Serbia	セルビア	serubia
Slovakia	スロバキア	surobakia

Croatia	クロアチア	kuroachia
The Czech Republic	チェコ	cheko
Estonia	エストニア	esutonia
Bosnia-Herzegovina	ボスニア	bosunia.
	・ヘルツェゴヴィナ	herutsegovina
Macedonia	マケドニア地方	makedonia chihō

Slovenia	スロヴェニア	surovenia
Montenegro	モンテネグロ	monteneguro
Belarus	ベラルーシー	bera rūshī
Moldavia	モルドヴァ	morudova
Russia	ロシア	roshia
Ukraine	ウクライナ	ukuraina

COUNTRIES OF THE WORLD. PART 2

Asia	アジア	ajia
Vietnam	ベトナム	betonamu
India	インド	indo
Israel	イスラエル	isuraeru
China	中国	chūgoku
Lebanon	レバノン	rebanon
Mongolia	モンゴル	mongoru
Malaysia	マレーシア	marēshia
Pakistan	パキスタン	pakisutan
Saudi Arabia	サウジアラビア	saujiarabia
Thailand	タイ	tai
Taiwan	台湾	taiwan
Turkey	トルコ	toruko
Japan	日本	nippon
Afghanistan	アフガニスタン	afuganisutan
Bangladesh	バングラデシュ	banguradeshu
Indonesia	インドネシア	indoneshia
Jordan	ヨルダン	yorudan
Iraq	イラク	iraku
Iran	イラン	iran
Cambodia	カンボジア	kanbojia
Kuwait	クウェート	kuwēto
Laos	ラオス	raosu
Myanmar	ミャンマー	myanmā
Nepal	ネパール	nepāru
United Arab Emirates	アラブ首長国連邦	arabu shuchō koku renpō
Syria	シリア	shiria
Palestine	パレスチナ	paresuchina
South Korea	大韓民国	daikanminkoku
North Korea	北朝鮮	kitachōsen
United States of America	アメリカ合衆国	amerika gasshūkoku
Canada	カナダ	kanada
Mexico	メキシコ	mekishiko

Argentina	アルゼンチン	aruzenchin
Brazil	ブラジル	burajiru
Colombia	コロンビア	koronbia
Cuba	キューバ	kyūba
Chile	チリ	chiri
Venezuela	ベネズエラ	benezuera
Ecuador	エクアドル	ekuadoru

The Bahamas	バハマ	bahama
Panama	パナマ	panama
Egypt	エジプト	ejiputo
Morocco	モロッコ	morokko
Tunisia	チュニジア	chunijia

Kenya	ケニア	kenia
Libya	リビア	ribia
South Africa	南アフリカ	minamiafurika
Australia	オーストラリア	ōsutoraria
New Zealand	ニュージーランド	nyūjīrando

WEATHER. NATURAL DISASTERS

weather	天気	tenki
weather forecast	天気予報	tenki yohō
temperature	温度	ondo
thermometer	温度計	ondo kei
barometer	気圧計	kiatsu kei
sun	太陽	taiyō
to shine (vi)	眩しい	mabushii
sunny (day)	晴れの	hare no
to come up (vi)	昇る	noboru
to set (vi)	落ちる	ochiru
rain	雨	ame
it's raining	雨が降っている	ame ga futte iru
pouring rain	土砂降り	doshaburi
rain cloud	嵐雲	arashi kumo
puddle	水たまり	mizutamari
to get wet (in rain)	濡れる	nureru
thunderstorm	雷雨	raiu
lightning (~ strike)	稲妻	inazuma
to flash (vi)	ピカッと光る	pikatto hikaru
thunder	雷	kaminari
it's thundering	雷が鳴っている	kaminari ga natte iru
hail	あられ	arare
it's hailing	ひょうが降っている	hyou ga futte iru
heat (of summer)	猛暑	mōsho
it's hot	暑い	atsui
it's warm	暖かい	atatakai
it's cold	寒い	samui
mist (fog)	霧	kiri
misty (adj)	霧の	kiri no
cloud	雲	kumo
cloudy (adj)	曇りの	kumori no
humidity	湿気	shikke
snow	雪	yuki
it's snowing	雪が降っている	yuki ga futte iru
heavy frost	厳寒	genkan

below zero (adv)	零下	reika
hoarfrost	霜	shimo
bad weather	悪い天気	warui tenki

disaster	災害	saigai
flood	洪水	kōzui
avalanche	雪崩	nadare
earthquake	地震	jishin

tremor, quake	震動	shindō
epicenter	震央	shinō
eruption	噴火	funka
lava	溶岩	yōgan

tornado	颶風	gufū
twister	たつまき	tatsumaki
hurricane	ハリケーン	harikēn
tsunami	津波	tsunami
cyclone	サイクロン	saikuron

ANIMALS. PART 1

| animal | 動物 | dōbutsu |
| predator | 捕食者 | hoshoku sha |

tiger	虎	tora
lion	ライオン	raion
wolf	オオカミ	ōkami
fox	狐	kitsune
jaguar	ジャガー	jagā

lynx	オオヤマネコ	ooyamaneko
coyote	コヨーテ	koyōte
jackal	ジャッカル	jakkaru
hyena	ハイエナ	haiena

squirrel	栗鼠	risu
hedgehog	針鼠	harinezumi
rabbit	兎	usagi
raccoon	洗熊	arai kuma

hamster	ハムスター	hamusutā
mole	モグラ	mogura
mouse	鼠	nezumi
rat	ラット	ratto
bat	こうもり	kōmori

beaver	ビーバー	bībā
horse	馬	uma
deer	鹿	shika
camel	ラクダ	rakuda
zebra	縞馬	shimauma

whale	鯨	kujira
seal	海豹	kaihyō
walrus	海象	seiuchi
dolphin	海豚	iruka

bear	熊	kuma
monkey	猿	saru
elephant	象	zō
rhinoceros	犀	sai
giraffe	キリン	kirin

hippopotamus	河馬	kaba
kangaroo	カンガルー	kangarū
cat	猫	neko
dog	犬	inu

cow	雌牛	meushi
bull	雄牛	o ushi
sheep	羊	hitsuji
goat	山羊	yagi

donkey	驢馬	roba
pig	豚	buta
hen (chicken)	鶏	niwatori
rooster	雄鳥	ondori

duck	アヒル	ahiru
goose	鵞鳥	gachō
turkey (hen)	七面鳥	shichimenchō
sheepdog	牧羊犬	bokuyō ken

ANIMALS. PART 2

bird	鳥	tori
pigeon	鳩	hato
sparrow	雀	suzume
tit	四十雀	shijūkara
magpie	鵲	kasasagi

eagle	鷲	washi
hawk	鷹	taka
falcon	隼	hayabusa

swan	白鳥	shiratori
crane	鶴	tsuru
stork	シュバシコウ	shubashikou
parrot	鸚鵡	ōmu
peacock	孔雀	kujaku
ostrich	駝鳥	dachō

heron	鷺	sagi
nightingale	サヨナキドリ	sayonakidori
swallow	燕	tsubame
woodpecker	キツツキ	kitsutsuki
cuckoo	郭公	kakkō
owl	梟	fukurō

penguin	ペンギン	pengin
tuna	鮪	maguro
trout	鱒	masu
eel	鰻	unagi

shark	サメ	same
crab	蟹、カニ	kani, kani
jellyfish	クラゲ	kurage
octopus	たこ	tako

starfish	海星	kaisei
sea urchin	海胆、海栗	uni, umi kuri
seahorse	竜の落とし子	ryū no otoshi ko
shrimp	小エビ	koebi
snake	蛇	hebi
viper	クサリヘビ	kusarihebi
lizard	蜥蜴	tokage

iguana	イグアナ	iguana
chameleon	カメレオン	kamereon
scorpion	サソリ	sasori
turtle	亀	kame
frog	蛙	kaeru
crocodile	鰐	wani
insect, bug	昆虫	konchū
butterfly	蝶	chō
ant	蟻	ari
fly	蠅	hae
mosquito	蚊	ka
beetle	甲虫	kabutomushi
bee	蜂	hachi
spider	蜘蛛	kumo

TREES. PLANTS

tree	木	ki
birch	白樺	shirakanba
oak	オーク	ōku
linden tree	科の木	shinanoki
aspen	ヤマナラシ	yamanarashi
maple	楓	kaede
spruce	トウヒ属	touhi zoku
pine	松	matsu
cedar	ヒマラヤスギ	himarayasugi
poplar	ポプラ	popura
rowan	ナナカマド	nanakamado
beech	ブナ	buna
elm	ニレ	nire
ash (tree)	トネリコ	toneriko
chestnut	栗	kuri
palm tree	椰子	yashi
bush	低木	teiboku
mushroom	茸	take
toadstool	毒キノコ	doku kinoko
boletus	ポルチーニ	poruchīni
russula	ベニタケ	benitake
fly agaric	テングタケ属	tengu take zoku
death cap	毒茸	dokutake
flower	花	hana
bouquet (of flowers)	花束	hanataba
rose (flower)	バラ	bara
tulip	チューリップ	chūrippu
carnation	カーネーション	kānēshon
camomile	カモミール	kamomīru
cactus	サボテン	saboten
lily of the valley	スズラン	suzuran
snowdrop	スノードロップ	sunōdoroppu
water lily	睡蓮	suiren
tropical greenhouse	温室	onshitsu
grass lawn	芝生	shibafu

| flowerbed | 花壇 | kadan |
| plant | 植物 | shokubutsu |

grass	草	kusa
leaf	葉	ha
petal	花びら	hanabira
stem	茎	kuki
young plant (shoot)	幼芽	yō me

cereals (plants)	穀物	kokumotsu
wheat	小麦	komugi
rye	ライ麦	raimugi
oats	カラスムギ	karasumugi

millet	黍	kibi
barley	大麦	ōmugi
corn	トウモロコシ	tōmorokoshi
rice	米	bei

VARIOUS USEFUL WORDS

balance (of situation)	衡平	kōhei
base (basis)	基礎	kiso
beginning	始め	hajime
category	カテゴリー	kategorī
choice	選択	sentaku
coincidence	一致	icchi
comparison	比較	hikaku
degree (extent, amount)	程度	teido
development	発達	hattatsu
difference	差異	sai
effect (e.g., of drugs)	効果	kōka
effort (exertion)	努力	doryoku
element	要素	yōso
example (illustration)	例	rei
fact	事実	jijitsu
help	手伝い	tetsudai
ideal	理想	risō
kind (sort, type)	種目	shumoku
mistake, error	間違い	machigai
moment	瞬間	shunkan
obstacle	障害	shōgai
part (~ of sth)	一部	ichibu
pause (break)	休止	kyūshi
position	位置	ichi
problem	問題	mondai
process	過程	katei
progress	進歩	shinpo
property (quality)	性質	seishitsu
reaction	反応	hannō
risk	危険	kiken
secret	秘密	himitsu
series	シリーズ	shirīzu
shape (outer form)	形状	keijō

situation	状況	jōkyō
solution	解決	kaiketsu
standard (adj)	標準的な	hyōjun teki na
stop (pause)	休止	kyūshi
style	スタイル	sutairu
system	システム	shisutemu

table (chart)	表	hyō
tempo, rate	テンポ	tenpo
term (word, expression)	用語	yōgo
truth	真実	shinjitsu
turn (please wait your ~)	順番	junban

urgent (adj)	至急の	shikyū no
utility (usefulness)	実用性	jitsuyō sei
variant (alternative)	オプション	opushon
way (means, method)	方法	hōhō
zone	地帯	chitai

MODIFIERS. ADJECTIVES. PART 1

additional (adj)	追加の	tsuika no
ancient (~ civilization)	古代の	kodai no
artificial (adj)	人工の	jinkō no
bad (adj)	悪い	warui
beautiful (person)	美しい	utsukushii
big (in size)	大きな	ōkina
bitter (taste)	苦い	nigai
blind (sightless)	盲目の	mōmoku no
central (adj)	中心の	chūshin no
children's (adj)	子供の	kodomo no
clandestine (secret)	秘密の	himitsu no
clean (free from dirt)	クリーン	kurīn
clever (smart)	利口な	rikō na
compatible (adj)	適合する	tekigō suru
contented (adj)	満足した	manzoku shi ta
continuous (adj)	連続的な	renzoku teki na
dangerous (adj)	危険な	kiken na
dead (not alive)	死んだ	shin da
dense (fog, smoke)	濃い	koi
difficult (decision)	難い	katai
dirty (not clean)	汚い	kitanai
easy (not difficult)	易しい	yasashii
empty (glass, room)	空の	sora no
exact (amount)	正確な	seikaku na
excellent (adj)	立派な	rippa na
excessive (adj)	過度の	kado no
exterior (adj)	外部の	gaibu no
fast (quick)	速い	hayai
fertile (land, soil)	肥えた	koe ta
fragile (china, glass)	ワレモノ	waremono
free (at no cost)	無料の	muryō no
fresh (~ water)	淡水の	tansui no
frozen (food)	冷凍の	reitō no
full (completely filled)	満ちた	michi ta

happy (adj)	幸福な	kōfuku na
hard (not soft)	硬い	katai
huge (adj)	巨大な	kyodai na
ill (sick, unwell)	病気の	byōki no
immobile (adj)	不動の	fudō no
important (adj)	重要な	jūyō na
interior (adj)	内部の	naibu no
last (e.g., ~ week)	先...	sen ...
last (final)	最後の	saigo no
left (e.g., ~ side)	左の	hidari no
legal (legitimate)	合法の	gōhō no
light (in weight)	軽い	karui
liquid (fluid)	液状の	ekijō no
long (e.g., ~ way)	長い	nagai
loud (voice, etc.)	大きい	ōkii
low (voice)	低い	hikui

MODIFIERS. ADJECTIVES. PART 2

main (principal)	主な	omo na
matt (paint)	マット	matto
mysterious (adj)	謎の	nazo no
narrow (street, etc.)	狭い	semai
native (of country)	生まれた	umare ta
negative (adj)	否定の	hitei no
new (adj)	新しい	atarashii
next (e.g., ~ week)	来	ki
normal (adj)	標準的な	hyōjun teki na
not clear (adj)	明確でない	meikaku de nai
not difficult (adj)	むずかしくない	muzukashiku nai
obligatory (adj)	義務的な	gimu teki na
old (house)	古い	furui
open (adj)	開いた	hirai ta
opposite (adj)	反対	hantai
ordinary (usual)	普通の	futsū no
original (unusual)	独自	dokuji
personal (adj)	個人的な	kojin teki na
polite (adj)	礼儀正しい	reigi tadashii
poor (not rich)	貧乏な	binbō na
possible (adj)	可能な	kanō na
principal (main)	主な	omo na
probable (adj)	ありそうな	ari sō na
public (open to all)	公共の	kōkyō no
rare (adj)	珍しい	mezurashii
raw (uncooked)	生の	nama no
right (not left)	右の	migi no
ripe (fruit)	熟れた	ure ta
risky (adj)	危険な	kiken na
sad (~ look)	哀しい	kanashii
second hand (adj)	中古	chūko
shallow (water)	浅い	asai
sharp (blade, etc.)	鋭い	surudoi
short (in length)	短い	mijikai
similar (adj)	に似て	ni ni te

small (in size)	小さい	chīsai
smooth (surface)	平滑	heikatsu
soft (to touch)	柔らかい	yawarakai
solid (~ wall)	頑丈な	ganjō na
sour (flavor, taste)	酸っぱい	suppai
spacious (house, etc.)	広い	hiroi
special (adj)	特別の	tokubetsu no
straight (line, road)	直...	choku ...
strong (person)	強い	tsuyoi
stupid (foolish)	愚かな	oroka na
superb, perfect (adj)	優れた	sugure ta
sweet (sugary)	甘い	amai
tan (adj)	日焼けした	hiyake shi ta
tasty (adj)	美味しい	oishii

VERBS. PART 1

to accuse (vt)	告訴する	kokuso suru
to agree (say yes)	承知する	shōchi suru
to announce (vt)	アナウンス	anaunsu
to answer (vi, vt)	回答する	kaitō suru
to apologize (vi)	謝る	ayamaru
to arrive (vi)	到着する	tōchaku suru
to ask (~ oneself)	問う	tou
to be absent	欠席する	kesseki suru
to be afraid	怖がる	kowagaru
to be born	生まれる	umareru
to be in a hurry	急ぐ	isogu
to beat (dog, person)	打つ	utsu
to begin (vt)	始める	hajimeru
to believe (in God)	信じる	shinjiru
to belong to …	所有する	shoyū suru
to break (split into pieces)	折る	oru
to build (vt)	建設する	kensetsu suru
to buy (purchase)	買う	kau
can (v aux)	出来る	dekiru
can (v aux)	できる	dekiru
to cancel (call off)	取り消す	torikesu
to catch (vt)	捕らえる	toraeru
to change (vt)	変える	kaeru
to check (to examine)	検査する	kensa suru
to choose (select)	選ぶ	erabu
to clean (tidy)	掃除する	sōji suru
to close (vt)	閉める	shimeru
to compare (vt)	比較する	hikaku suru
to complain (vi, vt)	不平を言う	fuhei o iu
to confirm (vt)	確認する	kakunin suru
to congratulate (vt)	祝う	iwau
to cook (dinner)	調理する	chōri suru
to copy (vt)	コピーする	kopī suru
to cost (vt)	かかる	kakaru
to count (add up)	計算する	keisan suru

to count on ...	当て込む	atekomu
to create (vt)	作る	tsukuru
to cry (weep)	泣く	naku
to dance (vi, vt)	踊る	odoru
to deceive (vi, vt)	だます	damasu
to decide (~ to do sth)	決定する	kettei suru
to delete (vt)	削除する	sakujo suru
to demand (request firmly)	要求する	yōkyū suru
to deny (vt)	否定する	hitei suru
to depend on ...	…に依存する	... ni izon suru
to despise (vt)	軽蔑する	keibetsu suru
to die (vi)	死ぬ	shinu
to dig (vt)	掘る	horu
to disappear (vi)	消える	kieru
to discuss (vt)	討議する	tōgi suru
to disturb (vt)	邪魔する	jama suru
to dive (vi)	潜る	moguru
to divorce (vi)	離婚する	rikon suru

VERBS. PART 2

to do (vt)	する	suru
to doubt (have doubts)	疑う	utagau
to drink (vi, vt)	飲む	nomu
to drop (let fall)	落とす	otosu
to dry (clothes, hair)	乾かす	kawakasu
to eat (vi, vt)	食べる	taberu
to end (e.g., relationship)	終わる	owaru
to excuse (forgive)	許す	yurusu
to exist (vi)	存在する	sonzai suru
to expect (foresee)	見越す	mikosu
to explain (vt)	説明する	setsumei suru
to fall (vi)	倒れる	taoreru
to fight (vi)	けんかする	kenka suru
to find (vt)	見つける	mitsukeru
to finish (vt)	終わる	owaru
to fly (vi)	飛ぶ	tobu
to forbid (vt)	禁ずる	kinzuru
to forget (vi, vt)	忘れる	wasureru
to forgive (vt)	許す	yurusu
to get tired	疲れる	tsukareru
to give (vt)	手渡す	tewatasu
to go (on foot)	行く	iku
to hate (vt)	憎む	nikumu
to have (vt)	持つ	motsu
to have breakfast	朝食をとる	chōshoku o toru
to have dinner	夕食をとる	yūshoku o toru
to have lunch	昼食をとる	chūshoku o toru
to hear (vt)	聞く	kiku
to help (vt)	手伝う	tetsudau
to hide (vt)	隠す	kakusu
to hope (vi, vt)	望む	nozomu
to hunt (vi, vt)	狩る	karu
to hurry (vi)	急ぐ	isogu
to insist (vi, vt)	主張する	shuchō suru
to insult (vt)	侮辱する	bujoku suru

to invite (vt)	招待する	shōtai suru
to joke (vi)	冗談を言う	jōdan o iu
to keep (vt)	保つ	tamotsu
to kill (vt)	殺す	korosu
to know (sb)	知っている	shitte iru
to know (sth)	知る	shiru
to like (I like ...)	好む	konomu
to look at ...	...を見る	... o miru
to lose (umbrella, etc.)	なくす	nakusu
to love (sb)	愛する	aisuru
to make a mistake	誤る	ayamaru
to meet (vi, vt)	...に会う	... ni au
to miss (school, etc.)	欠席する	kesseki suru

VERBS. PART 3

to obey (vi, vt)	従う	shitagau
to open (vt)	開ける	akeru
to participate (vi)	参加する	sanka suru
to pay (vi, vt)	払う	harau
to permit (vt)	許可する	kyoka suru
to play (children)	遊ぶ	asobu
to pray (vi, vt)	祈る	inoru
to promise (vt)	約束する	yakusoku suru
to propose (vt)	提案する	teian suru
to prove (vt)	証明する	shōmei suru
to read (vi, vt)	読む	yomu
to receive (vt)	受け取る	uketoru
to rent (sth from sb)	借りる	kariru
to repeat (say again)	繰り返して言う	kurikaeshi te iu
to reserve, to book	予約する	yoyaku suru
to run (vi)	走る	hashiru
to save (rescue)	救出する	kyūshutsu suru
to say (~ thank you)	言う	iu
to see (vt)	見る	miru
to sell (vt)	売る	uru
to send (vt)	送る	okuru
to shoot (vi)	撃つ	utsu
to shout (vi)	叫ぶ	sakebu
to show (vt)	見せる	miseru
to sign (document)	署名する	shomei suru
to sing (vi)	囀る	saezuru
to sit down (vi)	座る	suwaru
to smile (vi)	微笑む	hohoemu
to speak (vi, vt)	話す	hanasu
to steal (money, etc.)	盗む	nusumu
to stop (cease)	止める	tomeru
to study (vt)	学ぶ	manabu
to swim (vi)	泳ぐ	oyogu
to take (vt)	取る	toru
to talk to ...	...と話す	... to hanasu
to tell (story, joke)	話す	hanasu

to thank (vt)	感謝する	kansha suru
to think (vi, vt)	思う	omou
to translate (vt)	訳文する	yakubun suru
to trust (vt)	信用する	shinyō suru
to try (attempt)	試みる	kokoromiru
to turn (~ to the left)	曲がる	magaru
to turn off	消す	kesu
to turn on	つける	tsukeru
to understand (vt)	理解する	rikai suru
to wait (vt)	待つ	matsu
to want (wish, desire)	欲する	hossuru
to work (vi)	働く	hataraku
to write (vt)	書く	kaku

CONCLUSION

In conclusion, we will present a brief summary of all of the ideas we've tried to convey in this book:

- Create your own set of study materials. This can include textbooks, reference books, videos, printed and electronic books, topical dictionaries, computer programs, movie subtitles, phrasebooks, guidebooks, etc. It's best to assemble these materials right away, deliberately, rather than randomly putting them together during your studies.

- Even before you begin actively studying, try to obtain useful information about the foreign language. It's helpful to read about the history of the country or countries where the language is spoken.

- Create a list of the language's 1,500 most important words. These words will be your initial vocabulary. You need to learn them at the very beginning.

- Pick out several foreign movies and shows in the original language. They must be accompanied by subtitles in the original language. Try to find these subtitles as text. Movies and shows can give you the greatest set of learning material: video, audio, and text.

- Create your own word database and add all the new words you encounter during your studies. This will make it easy for you to learn and review new words.

- Read more. At the beginning stage, you can read children's books and adapted books; at later stages, you can read from the Internet, newspapers, magazines, and books in the original.

- Review your entire vocabulary as often as possible. Try to make an audio recording of every word. Then reviewing them won't take much time and energy from you.

We hope this book has been useful and will help you create an orderly system of independent study. Anybody can learn a foreign language quite well. All you need is the right set of study materials and to be able to use them effectively.

Good luck!

T&P Books Publishing

FOREIGN LANGUAGE

How to use modern technology to effectively learn foreign languages

Special edition for students of Japanese language

Created by Andrey Taranov
Layout by Studio 1•2•3 Books
Director Alis Morgunova

ISBN 978-1-78314-812-7

www.tpbooks.com

www.ingramcontent.com/pod-product-compliance
Lightning Source LLC
Chambersburg PA
CBHW071459070426
42452CB00041B/1931